CAY GARCIA

Behind Palace Walls

❦

In the service of a Saudi princess

TAFELBERG

This book is dedicated to my sister.
For your ongoing support in all that I do, your
unconditional love and for being there for me no matter
what. My love and respect for you knows no bounds.

Tafelberg,
an imprint of NB Publishers,
a division of Media24 Boeke (Pty) Ltd,
40 Heerengracht, Cape Town, South Africa
PO Box 6525, Roggebaai, 8012, South Africa
www.tafelberg.com

Text © Cay Garcia (2014)

Cover design: Nic Jooste
Book design: Nazli Jacobs
E-book design: Nazli Jacobs
Editing: Anna Rich
Proofreading: Julie Miller
E-book checking: Lorraine Braid

Printed and bound by Interpak Books, Pietermaritzburg
Product group from well-managed forests and other controlled sources.

First edition 2014, second impression 2014
ISBN: 978-0-624-06602-6

Epub edition: 978-0-624-06603-3
Mobi edition: 978-0-624-06604-0

PROLOGUE

The beginning of the end

⁙

IT IS two o' clock in the morning. The sandstorm is at its peak. The windows are rattling as if someone is hammering on them. The desert sand, like talcum powder, penetrates even though everything is tightly shut. It hangs in the air making breathing difficult.

The noise is unsettling. I am alone at home.

There's a light knock on my bedroom door. My flat mate, Mona, who works in the same palace and has just returned from work, hands me a large envelope. She seems flustered as she relays the news, "You have to be out of the country today!" Her tension is evident in her shallow, rapid breathing, but the excitement in her eyes confirms my suspicion that there is much riding on this for her.

The envelope contains a flight ticket and an exit permit. This, at the whim of a princess who doesn't have a clue what's really going on beyond her bedroom door. Although I knew this was coming – and asked for it even – I reel at the finality. A flood of adrenalin propels me out of bed. I run two doors

— 5 —

down into a wall of sand, to what has become my island in a storm.

We agree to stay awake the whole night and treasure the time left together. Exhilarating but utterly draining shows of emotion have us falling into an exhausted sleep at six in the morning.

Suddenly it is 10 o'clock. I feel bereft at the 11 hours left. The enormity of what I have to get done floors me and, quite frankly, I don't know where to start.

The rest of the day plays off in slow motion, yet time has never moved faster. As I pack, I try to make sense of it all. Every surface is piled with clothes, beautiful pieces of material and artwork collected over the past four months. Six hours till take-off.

Decisions

IT'S A beautiful Saturday afternoon as I drive to work – not a cloud in the sky, not a breath of wind. A day that begs for a long walk on any beach around the Cape peninsula or a breathtaking mountain or forest trail.

As I turn into the largest mall in the southern hemisphere, where I work, I'm amazed at the volume of traffic at every entrance, queues wrapped halfway round the block. Inside, people scurry like ants. The noise is deafening. I feel a surge of frustration and restlessness and my mind rages with the thought that surely to God there must be more to life than this!

Roughly a month later, after careful deliberation, I resign from my job and enrol in a fulltime, 10-week butling course. I'm not sure if my brain is still capable of studying at my comparatively advanced age but the qualification is internationally recognised and promises great opportunities of work in any corner of the world, not to mention pretty substantial salaries and perks. I have no dependants and the idea of doing something this outrageous at my age only adds to the excitement.

The demand for the excellence that butlers offer increases every year, as more and more people reach millionaire status. The idea that one person can manage their staff, mansions, fleet of cars and holiday homes has caught on as it is an attractive alternative to having short term staff from dubious agencies.

The statement on the website that the course is intensive and exhausting is no lie. But it fails to mention that it is also the most fun you can have with your clothes on.

On day one, everyone is on time. We are issued with three intimidating manuals, black bowties and white gloves. Throughout the course we are required to wear black suits, crisp white shirts and a bowtie. Trying to keep it straight is an ongoing challenge.

At the first military-style line-up outside the Academy, white gloves donned, I revel in the chaos as students rush to please without really having a clue what to do. We all feel proud but the reason escapes us at this early stage. Strangers become friends and allies.

Our principal, Mr Van Wyk, an attractive man in his early thirties, takes us under his wing as we clumsily try to follow his instructions. Not only is he an expert in his field, but he has the experience to match; he has been butler to presidents and international celebrities – so who are we to argue about his tried and tested methods? We are all in awe. And, I might add, terrified.

Our class guardian, Mr Fourie, initially comes across like a Machiavellian character from *The Godfather* but we soon discover that he has a heart the size of Manhattan. He is relentless in his quest to turn us into professional butlers. He spots little things – never again will I leave the table without pushing in my chair.

The third person in this dynamic trio is Mr Lewis, the recruitment agent and photographer. His sense of humour knows no bounds and we love him. He puts us through rigorous Skype interviews conducted from his office while we face a monitor in front of the class, trying to answer questions like, "Are you arrogant?"

We cover Silver Service; handling a fork and spoon is child's play with bare hands – but with gloves on, we're soon on all fours retrieving objects we have dropped from dark corners.

As part of the different dining ceremonies, we cover Russian service, French service, family service and the correct etiquette for a buffet, to mention just a few. My favourite is the graceful art of "Ballet of Service", which they do at Buckingham Palace.

At this stage, no one can balance a tray with anything larger than a matchbox on it. We stand with books balanced on our heads as six long-stemmed champagne flutes are filled with water and placed on our trays. Our wide eyes give us away – panick reigns supreme – but no one breaks a glass. Yet.

Wardrobe management is next; we learn how to colour code, to separate clothing according to its function and season, and everything else besides, from caring for furs to polishing and placing shoes onto shoe horns. We pack and unpack a suit-case until we can do it in our sleep. A suit jacket may be kept in a suitcase for up to three months and, if packed cor-rectly, it will not have a single crease. After three months? I think back to my last trip – to Italy – and my heap of crumpled clothes. I am seriously impressed.

We polish silver as part of housekeeping. We learn to poach eggs the French way and cook up delicious dishes like Crêpes Suzette – without burning down the Academy.

A barista shows us how to make spectacular espresso and cappuccino. Half the class focuses on his very tight jeans, thus failing to get the foam just right.

A master sommelier, one of only four in South Africa, teaches us the fine art of pouring, and pairing wine with food. To this day it irks me when a waiter pours wine without the label facing the diner – and this happens even in top restaurants. Perfection is part of the game. The wine tasting sessions cement the bonds between us students.

We write lengthy exams on food terminology, and words like puttanesca roll easily off our tongues.

During our mixology lessons, I'm delighted to find out how to fix a Manhattan iced-tea.

We set tea trays and spectacular tables. We arrange flowers and learn about cigars and cognac. We learn to serve vodka or champagne with caviar and its many accompanying dishes.

A security specialist alerts us to safety precautions. We became adept at operating automated security systems.

We are taught how to go green and made aware of how many ways there are to recycle.

There is not much this course does not cover.

Although we write tests that count towards our final grade every morning, there's a week-long series of exams.

After a gruelling 10 weeks we graduate and my darling sister flies down from Johannesburg. After listening, many a day, to my exhausted ramblings as I suffered from information overload, it was fitting for her to be there. My joy at seeing her walk the red carpet that night knows no bounds.

I receive my merit certificate for achieving above 80 percent! My brain feels foggy – on graduation night I come down with a cold that soon turns into a monster. It amazes me that my body has carried me through the last week of exams; I wouldn't have had the focus I needed to do well if the cold had hit earlier in the week. I am man-down for three days.

Now I'm in the hands of Mr Lewis, the recruitment agent who specialises in placing new graduates. Before long, I'm offered a job as PA and palace manager to a princess in the Royal House of Saud, in Riyadh, capital city of Saudi Arabia.

On a lazy Sunday afternoon, lying round the pool with friends, glass of chardonnay within reach, I read over the terms of the offer. A year-long contract in Saudi Arabia sounds magical to a brain stuck deeply in a rut. The recruitment agent tells me to expect a call from the prospective employer.

My phone is never far from my side.

Two days later, the phone shrills – and the number is foreign. I take a deep breath and answer. The conversation goes extremely well. I have been warned to address the princess by another name, one that she has provided, as she wishes to hide the fact that she is royalty. I play along.

"The climate is very dry. Do you feel you could live here for a year?" she asks. I assure her that I love a dry climate – I prefer it to intense humidity. I am tempted to add that in a dry climate every day is a good hair day. But I don't.

Next, she asks if I would have a problem disciplining staff. I measure my words, telling her in a nice way that if you treat your staff with respect, I believe you get more out of them. She doesn't much like my answer.

"I would have to discipline you from time to time as well, Mrs C."

I don't much like her tone but assure her that I'm not against constructive criticism. Though I do add: "As long as it is not in front of the staff I have to manage."

"Sometimes that cannot be helped, Mrs C," she replies.

At this point, warning bells should have rung.

I find it hard to believe that she has already made up her mind that she would have to discipline me "from time to time" even though she hasn't met me yet but I reassure myself that whatever happens, I will handle it then. It is not enough of a deterrent to taking up the position.

Two hours later, Mr Lewis calls.

I have been accepted.

Imagination soars

❦

I START researching the Magic Kingdom – anything I can get my hands on. I even hire *Lawrence of Arabia* – the movie and the documentary – from my local library to try to get the gist of what to expect in this fascinating country.

Riyadh is shrouded in mystery as no tourists are allowed in this holy city. There's no such thing as a tourist visa. "Infidels" (non-believers) are not allowed in unless they have a sponsor in the form of an employer. Expats can get special permits for their spouses. Although I find the restrictions alarming, I am deeply intrigued.

Expats are drawn here in spite of the austere lifestyle by the tax free salaries that are way above what can be earned at home, wherever home may be. Millions of expats from all over the world work in Saudi Arabia and embassy stats are that men outnumber women 50 to one. The irony does not escape me.

It is an adventure one cannot buy.

After I accept the offer, a German butler already in the employ of the princess phones me on her behalf. She fires questions at me in a gruff, abrasive voice. I fend them off with simple answers.

"Do you drink?" she asks.

"I live in one of the most enchanting wine regions in the world and grew up with wine, so yes, I do enjoy a glass of wine."

I assure her that I could live without it for a while, though. In time, it would become apparent that she likes a tipple herself. After an hour, the arrogant cross-examination, verging on verbal assault, abates. I'm exhausted.

Unbeknownst to me, I'd been on speaker phone.

The princess and I speak regularly on the phone. She has a slight American accent yet has never set foot in America. For the most part, she sounds utterly charming. There is no indication that she is bipolar.

Parts of my contract reflect the harsh regulations of the country. It states that I am not permitted any intimate relations.

During one of our many telephonic conversations, I ask Princess Arabella exactly what that clause means. She is quick to tell me that I may not become romantically involved while in her employ. One of her previous PAs met and married someone there and, for whatever reason, it did not work for the princess. I assure her it is the last thing on my mind – especially in her country.

Saudi Arabia is still under Sharia law, and Riyadh, the most conservative of the Saudi cities, doesn't much favour self-expression. The feared religious police, the mutawa, who are also known as the Committee for the Propagation of Virtue and the Prevention of Vice, lurk where you least expect them so it's wise to remain modest at all times.

The mutawa patrol streets and malls, and administer punishment to anyone accused of breaking the strict religious laws that subjugate women in particular – and nowhere as zealously as in Riyadh.

If the mutawa catch you having a conversation with a man who is not your husband or a relative, you will land in jail for prostitution.

If a man is linked with a Muslim woman who is not a family connection, rape charges are not uncommon and are punishable by death. Implications for the woman involved are severe. She is first taken to hospital to check whether her virginity is intact, then to jail. Should her virginity be in question, her male relatives decide on a punishment not always befitting the crime. By the hand of her father, brother or any other male relative, the woman can be stoned to death – an honour killing.

Proof of marital status as well as any move you make during

your contract – opening a bank account, buying a computer, registering a cell phone, incurring any traffic fines – comes in the form of an iqama, a credit card sized ID card. Smile for your iqama photo; you want a pleasant, harmless looking image for the authorities. When your contract ends, your iqama is thoroughly checked for any wrongdoing and money owed. Your employer will not grant you an exit visa – without which you cannot leave – unless your iqama is clear. That visa is much coveted by workers tired of abuse and yearning for home. So don't rattle ribs in Saudi.

Saudi Arabia applies the death penalty for a wide range of crimes including adultery, armed robbery, rejection of Islam, drug smuggling, kidnapping, rape, witchcraft and sorcery.

Previously, executions took place only on a Friday, the holy day, in public at what has become known as "Chop Chop Square" or Justice Square. People travel from far and wide to witness this. However, nowadays they happen any morning of the week.

I'd hear later from a fellow South African and her American boyfriend that they'd seen this for themselves. As a local man accused of drug trafficking was beheaded, they happened to pass the square. Locals brayed for justice as they fought for a better view. My friend was highly traumatised for weeks.

Saudi authorities make it clear to expats that if arrested, they are under no obligation to let their respective embassies know about the arrest, they are not entitled to a defence and they do not owe the alleged perpetrator a reason for the arrest. They may be convicted solely on the basis of "confessions" obtained under torture or other ill-treatment. By his own admission, Saudi's star executioner beheads over 2 500 people per year.

Preparations

❧

I EXPLODE into action, enthusiastically getting my preparations underway.

One week before my departure, the princess has a request. Would I be prepared to stay on in Cape Town for an extra month to take a yoga course so that I can give her lessons? Although a request, I cannot say no. Anyhow, I am secretly delighted as it affords me an extra month in Cape Town. I re-rent my garden cottage for a month.

The hunt for a yoga studio begins. My body has not seen exercise in a while, so, with great trepidation, I enrol. I give them brief details of what is needed and they work out a schedule for me. What I know about yoga is sketchy so on my first day, my instructor hands me some books on the subject and a very large manual to work through. I'm excited but uncertain I can do it. I decide to, quite literally, go with the flow.

My first class, Vinyāsa, takes me by surprise – I really enjoy it. My body feels light and supple the rest of the day. The next day my second class, Bikram – hot yoga – is sheer hell.

— 19 —

The heat is unbearable. Sweat pours down my face and drips off my chin. I come out drenched, wrenched and seeing stars. Apparently I am cleansed from the inside out. My glowing skin encourages me.

A month down the line, I'm a lot more agile, and wiser in the ways of the yogi. The manual had seemed insurmountable but I've worked through it from cover to cover. My test is to present a 15-minute class to the teachers while they critique me. I'm given the all clear. I'm good to go!

Between the many send-off parties with different groups of friends and the more sobering requirements for my visa – medicals, inoculations and police clearance – time blurs.

At the very last moment, I remove my belly ring, with its delicate cross, and replace it with a little ruby. We've come a long way and I feel quite naked without it. The princess has made it clear: Bibles and crosses are banned in the Magic Kingdom.

The journey

❦

STRAPPED IN, ready for the second leg of my journey from Johannesburg to Dubai, I wonder why my life has deviated so far off the well-trodden path. My new-found bravado is gone and for a moment I feel that my common sense has left with it. And in its place, I'm at the mercy of who knows what. The reality of what I'm about to take on hits home with the same force as the jet engines that lift me into the unknown. There is no turning back. I bow my head and ask God for protection – what from, I don't know, but I feel better for asking.

There is serious turbulence for the first two hours of the flight so service is postponed. This only adds to my unease – I'd intended to take advantage of the complimentary wine to still my mind and relieve my fear of flying. In Saudi, alcohol is strictly forbidden and if you're caught in possession of it, the penalty is fifty lashes and up to seven years in jail. Drug trafficking or possession carries the death penalty. No exceptions. Even for a little weed. For this very reason my friends laughingly rename Riyadh "Rehab".

Once we leave the turbulence behind, I'm pleased to see the drinks cart being wheeled down the aisle. I request two small bottles of red – you never know when they will come around again. Five hours into the eight-hour flight, I am hoping for sleep to overtake me but it doesn't. Poignant images of the many goodbyes said in the last weeks come to mind as the wine dulls the rough edges, and adds a rosy glow to my apprehension, which can't be a bad thing.

The landing at Dubai International is flawless. Stiffly, groggily, I make my way to the exit, to be hit by heat so intense it almost feels abrasive. I'd been noting the temperatures in the Middle East over the past two months, relieved that I was not arriving in July when temperatures hover round the mid forties. But I had not taken the humidity of Dubai into account.

It's early morning. I'm tired and bleary eyed. I have time to kill until my connecting flight to Riyadh in an hour. I'm conscious that I need to keep my wits about me. In no time at all, a sign flashing a final boarding call for my flight catches my eye. So much for keeping my wits about me. After asking how to get to gate 35, I am told it is a 15-minute walk from where I am standing, and half that at a run. I start to run.

My outsized handbag bought specially for travelling and the very heavy rucksack – complete with yoga manual – feel like a ball and chain bouncing painfully off my back as I zig-zag through the hordes. It will not make a good impression this early on if I can't get myself onto a connecting flight. It's just 6 o'clock yet the airport resembles Grand Central station at peak hour.

I am last on the bus. A couple of seconds later the doors hiss and we pull away from the terminal. People stare blatantly as I try to regain my breath. My near miss has jolted me awake and alert. My head throbs and the heat doesn't help, but I know I only have myself to blame.

I've chosen a window seat to take in every detail. I stare at the arid earth below. I need water. My eyes feel scratchy. Miles and miles of desert slip past. Riyadh appears on the horizon. From up here, everything looks devoid of colour. Just a drab yellow as far as the eye can see with drab buildings to match. Excitement surges through me.

The arrival

KING KHALID Airport feels like another planet. I am the only woman who isn't shrouded from head to toe in black. The aircon is set so high that even in my winter clothes, I am freezing.

It's not the majestic international airport I'd expected. What I see now falls terribly flat. The arrivals hall has a depressing look and a sombre mood hangs over the place.

I'm not too alarmed about looking so out of place as I have been assured that the princess's secretary will have an abaya for me at arrivals.

In Islamic countries, all parts of a woman's body that are awrah – not meant to be exposed – are covered by an abaya, an outer garment, and a hijab, a head scarf. In many of these countries, a woman's face is not considered awrah. But in Saudi Arabia, awrah includes every part of the body, besides hands and eyes, so most women are expected to wear a niqab, a veil over the face, as well.

There are several queues. The signage is in Arabic so I follow the people ahead of me. A man in a scary looking uniform strides up to me. His arrogant bearing makes me feel alarmed. Without making eye contact, he pulls my passport out of my hand. He says something in an urgent tone, still avoiding eye contact, and points to another queue. I'm relieved – it turns out he is just trying to help me.

At the last checkpoint, the official behind the counter looks at my passport, then at me, then back at my passport and says softly, "This is not a good photo." I have to agree, and I laugh with him. It was taken straight after graduation, when I was in the grip of severe flu, my eyes barely open – and the new rule of having to pull your hair back off the forehead doesn't help one bit. He is not a local. No Saudi man would make such a flippant comment.

After my photo and finger prints are taken, I make my way to the public arrivals hall. Among the throng of men waiting to pick up passengers, I expect to see the princess's secretary holding a board with my name on it. I scan the hall. After 30 minutes of hanging around, the crowd thins. Still no sign of the secretary.

That was my first lesson in Saudi time-keeping. If you are punctual, get over it; waiting is just part of Saudi life.

After an hour of wandering around, looking for someone

to claim me, I give up. I find a seat in the back row of a cluster of seats and take out my book.

I discreetly watch the comings and goings around me. I am fascinated. The crowds have thinned but the hostile stares haven't. Another hour passes.

Then I notice two men walking briskly in my direction. They stop right in front of me, towering over me, smelling strongly of cologne. "Passport!" says the taller one. I hand it over. They inspect it briefly then start walking away, summoning me to follow. Half relieved, half apprehensive, I scramble to get my luggage together and follow. That is the last I saw of my passport.

We walk into an underground parking area. I'm lagging behind, struggling with my luggage, still in Western clothes – no help is forthcoming and no abaya either. I am elegantly dressed in a long black and grey tailored skirt, a white shirt that lost some of its crispness somewhere over Africa, a red, black and grey paisley scarf and a black tailored jacket and black boots – only my hands and face bare. Yet the hostile stares continue. As my luggage is stowed in the boot, none too gently, and I'm ushered into the back seat, still not a word is uttered. The tint on the back windows is so dark that I can barely see out.

We leave the airport building and join the nightmarishly congested traffic. I'd read that 19 people die as a result of car accidents here every day. The reason Saudi has one of the highest accident rates in the world is immediately apparent – cars weave in and out of lanes at breakneck speed, passing with only a thumb's-width between side mirrors. Most drivers keep one hand on the hooter, the noise is grinding.

Reckless driving is part of the national identity. Wealthier men drag race high-end cars and the lower-classes "drift" their cars through traffic. These youngsters weave in and out between other cars while they intentionally over-steer, sometimes missing other drivers by a very small margin.

Saudi women are not allowed to drive – even though thousands own motor vehicles. The thinking is that they'd increase car accidents, they'd overcrowd the streets, they'd leave the house more often, their faces would be uncovered, and they'd interact with males, which would contribute to the erosion of traditional values. A leading Saudi cleric has even argued that women run the risk of damaging their ovaries and pelvises if they drive.

But not all Saudi women accept the ban on driving. In October last year, a handful drove through Riyadh in protest. They were arrested and released only after their male guardians signed statements that they would not drive again.

The women were suspended from their jobs, their passports were confiscated and they were forbidden from speaking to the press. About a year after the protest, they were permitted to return to work and their passports were returned. But they were kept under surveillance and passed over for promotions.

More recently, a few women used social media to publicise their cause. They got behind the wheel, filmed themselves, and uploaded the videos to YouTube.

Despite the alarming drive and dark windows, I manage to take in some of the surroundings.

The buildings thin and we seem to be heading straight into the desert. Doubt flares, my thoughts run wild. I'd expected the secretary to be a woman, accompanied by a male driver. Was I right to follow them? They speak in hushed tones, the older man in the passenger seat turning often to stare at me. I feel that I'm being assessed.

We reach what appears to be the edge of the city. I have my face plastered to the opaque window – I'm straining to see out, but it's also an attempt to avoid the old man's scrutiny. I am surprised at the ultra-modern buildings. The traffic does not let up.

At each green light, drivers further back honk at the cars

up front to hurry – they have only 40 seconds to make it through. Above each set of lights, a large digital screen counts down the seconds till the lights change. Red is allotted 160 seconds. I would often see one of our drivers nod off during the wait. They work long hours.

Home from home

FORTY MINUTES later, to my relief, we pull up outside a three-storey flat complex with very high walls. I am to share an apartment with Mona. She works for the same family – and was my interrogator during the telephonic interview. The driver helps me to the gate with my luggage, and shares one snippet of information with me as he wipes his face with a drenched hanky: 'Madam, is 45 degrees."

Three of Saudi Arabia's largest and most barren deserts border Riyadh. Summers are intensely hot, especially in the city where daytime temperatures sometimes reach over 49°C. The heat is constant. The only thing that makes it half bearable is that it is a dry heat.

He hands me a white box. The abaya.

I ring for Mona on the panel of numbers on the side of the gate. The heat beats down – and I'm still overdressed in my boots and winter gear. As we wait, I look round my new suburb. Cats lie under cars with their tongues protruding. They are listless and in terrible condition. I love cats, so I foresee a serious problem.

A full thirty five minutes later Mona opens the gate. I am melting in the heat. I ask her if she was sleeping. She wasn't. Thirty five minutes? Even the driver is clucking as he has had to wait with me.

Through the majestic wrought iron gate, there's a cluster of sand-coloured buildings. Most suburban buildings are painted shades of yellow to minimise cleaning – sand clings to everything. There is a sparkling pool with tables and chairs round it, and an undercover coffee station.

I later discover that at night this area is alive with music, animated chatter and laughter as residents smoke shisha pipes. In most compounds, there is a corner where people socialise until the early hours. At midday during the week, though, it is forlorn.

Lebanese bankers, interior designers, architects, American medics and English teachers make up this expat compound. Downtown housing tends to be taken by lower-salaried employees, both Saudi and expat. The compounds, depending on the owners and the cultural make-up of their residents, are much more liberal.

The bigger ones have restaurants, supermarkets, gyms, hairdressers and, of course, very active social clubs. Here, life is Western; you can walk around in shorts and a tank top if you wish. Some compounds are for Westerners only, with no Arabs allowed.

The flat is basic, nicely furnished and spacious. Cool air blasts off the walls. A couple of pictures and a pot plant or two will make it more homely. The fridge is stocked for my arrival and my flat mate is welcoming. I would soon find that sharing accommodation with a stranger for the first time since boarding school will stretch my creativity in keeping the peace. I excuse myself to take a quick shower.

Afterwards, I hang up my damp towels. Mona comes into the bathroom after me and straightens them so that they all line up precisely. Though I feel slightly disgruntled, I decide to let it go for now.

Mona is waiting with coffee as I join her at the kitchen table. She briefs me on protocol and hands me a four-page list of instructions to remember. I'm not taking in much – I'm exhausted and hot. Even though the interior is cool, it takes a while to shake the heat from outside. With a proud, smug smile, Mona confesses to being obsessive-compulsive. So that explains her need to straighten my towels.

The princess wants to meet me at six this evening. I need sleep to string a sentence together. I eventually crash for two hours.

My eyes are bloodshot. I shower again. Even in the coolness of my bedroom, the abaya feels stifling and far too long. Only the tips of my fingers stick out and fabric is gathered round my feet, inviting a fall.

The driver who collected me at the airport meets us at the compound gate. Mona has been instructed to accompany me. It is dusk, and Riyadh looks almost magical. Most of the buildings are lit with coloured lights. I feel as if I am looking in on someone else's life, like I've shaken a kaleidoscope to find new sounds, sights and smells.

The landscape is completely flat. At home, mountains or hills help me find my bearings. Here, the drivers take different routes to and from work each day, so it takes weeks before some areas become familiar. Mona tells me it is done deliberately for security reasons. I still can't fathom why they feel this is necessary.

On the way to the palace, Mona gives me last-minute instructions on how to stand when addressing royalty. I am not to sit before the princess does and when I walk out, I am not to turn my back on her. I make a mental note to lift my abaya off the floor and wish I'd had time to practice walking backwards.

I scan the protocol list again in the hope of remembering at least half of it before meeting the Princess.

Protocol

❦

IN THE PRESENCE OF ROYALTY

Whenever any Member of the Royal Family approaches, even children, you must rise if sitting down or move out of the way if you are standing up.

When you are busy and a Member of the Royal family approaches, stop and stand still and wait for permission to continue.

Address the Royals as following, Male – Your Highness or Prince or Amir. Female – Your Highness or Princess or Amira.

Do not walk in front of any Member of the Royal family. Either wait for them to pass or walk beside them ONLY if you are in a conversation with them.

If any Royalty comes down or goes up the stairs and you are already on the stairs, stand still, greet them and wait for them to pass then proceed.

If a Royal approaches a closed door, open the door, let them pass and disappear from sight before closing the door behind them.

If more than one Royal is walking together, there is a hierarchy from the most senior to the youngest. Greet the most senior first.

Never show your back to a Royal.

Knock before entering and wait for permission to enter.

EXPECTATIONS

Respect the Royals' space, do not crowd them.

Do special things for your Employer.

Make things pretty and attractive for your Employer.

Do not take things personally.

You are allowed to eat on invitation from a Royal or when the Royals have finished their meals.

BEHAVIOUR

Do not chew gum when talking to a Royal.

Do not bring anything to eat or drink when accompanying a Royal.

NOTE – *"Never put lip-ice on in front of royalty" should be added.*

Be meticulous in everything you do.

Respect the rules and laws of the country.

Be polite at all times.

Be discreet at all times.

Maintain a fine line between friendship and professionalism.

When speaking to a Royal on the phone, wait for the Royal to hang up first.

Do not interrupt a Royal member.

Never give instructions to a Royal.

Do not gossip.

Do not lie.

Do not talk unless spoken to.

Do not yap nonstop.

Do not raise your voice to a Royal in anger or discontent even if they are wrong. Wait for them to calm down before talking to them.

Do not answer back or be rude.

Do not nag or complain.

Do not show obsessive behaviour.

You are not allowed to have a buddy-buddy relationship with the other employees.

You are not allowed to have a relationship with a driver.

You are not allowed any intimate relationships whilst on contract in Saudi Arabia.

WHEN ACCOMPANYING A ROYAL

Be ready first wearing your abaya and be on standby, holding the Princess's abaya for when she is ready.

When accompanying a Royal, make sure the driver is informed and that the car is ready and waiting at the departure point.

Check with the gate that the driver is ready and waiting beside the car.

Ensure there is water in the car.

If the driver is not there, open and close the car door for the Royal.

Do not get into the car before the Royal is seated.

When alone with a Royal in the car, you sit in the back on the left hand side. Should there be another person with the Royal, you will sit in front with your head covered by your hijab.

Do not make frivolous and unnecessary conversation.

Make sure you smell good being in such close proximity of a Royal.

THE FOLLOWING TRAITS ARE DESIRED

Positive attitude

Understanding

Empathetic

Gentle

Caring

Loving

Compassionate

Contained

Patient

Stable

Balanced

Calm and Relaxed

Not temperamental

Not moody

Fun

Sense of humour

Know your place

Not arrogant

Not snobbish

Organised

Modern

Stylish

Class

Creative

Be well informed

The palace

❦

WE PULL up to gates easily six metres high. Ornate brass and stainless steel make up the elaborate and intricate design. The doorman swings the gates open. He looks like Moses in a kiddies' Bible – a messy beard hangs down to his chest. His name is Eli.

The palace grounds look spectacular as skilfully placed lights highlight the trees and shrubs and garden beds glow in the dark. The driveway curves around a Gothic fountain then splits into two around the majestic building straight ahead – the main palace. We walk the rest of the way over immaculate cobbled walkways adorned with tranquil water features. There is a strange but pleasant scent in the hot evening air that I can't quite identify.

The main palace guards the foreground of the vast property while four five-storey villas, one for each child, form a half moon behind it. The gardens are beautiful but I am surprised that so many of the shrubs and flowers are plastic. They are clustered in places where shrubs struggle to grow. Two pools, one heated, dominate the centre of the garden, a favourite area in spring and autumn for dinners.

Halfway through the property, a high wall separates the quarters where the drivers and other male staff live. Sixteen garages for the royal car collection cover the left perimeter of the property and a mosque is situated to the right. Five times a day my princess's father, the Amir, makes his way to this area, which is forbidden to women.

I will only meet the Amir once during my time at the palace. During my second week, while checking on the princess's newly planted herb garden, he catches me unawares on his way to the mosque.

I am in casual clothes, with bare shoulders and not yet aware that when the Amir is present a woman's head is required to be covered by the hijab. Once I realise this, I understand why all the servants from the main palace always have their hijabs draped around their necks.

Still, he is polite. He simply asks me who I am. I put my hands behind my back and reply that I am new to princess Arabella's staff. He gives a slight smile, nods and resumes his journey.

He is a handsome and dignified man in his forties who carries himself well. Even though he doesn't introduce himself, I somehow know that this is the royal patriarch. He has presence. I will come to learn that most of the staff are terrified of him.

I hear a strange noise coming from some shrubs at the side of the villa. A tiny kitten peeks out at me; its eyes are watery and speak of such suffering. I go over to pet the poor little thing but it runs away. I am shocked to see how thin and mangy it looks.

Mona explains that there are about seven cats on the palace grounds but feeding them is forbidden as they are there to catch rats. This kitten can't be more than a couple of weeks old! I make a mental note to bring some cat pellets with me; while I'm around, no animal will be starved.

We are met at the double wooden doors by a Filipino woman, her small frame emphasised by the enormity of the entrance. She offers us something to drink and shows us into the lounge. The furniture is garish. Glitzy, Liberace-style frilly cushions in different shades of yellow and purple crowd the couches, so that we are only able to sit on the edge of our seats. We are on time so we wait.

Murals of sunsets in yellow tones fill the walls from floor to ceiling. A little radio in the corner blasts out prayers – nonstop, monotonous, tuneless. Mona reminds me again that we are paid to wait.

Almost an hour passes. Keeping my eyes open is a fight without any distraction – conversation between Mona and I has long since dried up. Eventually we are summoned upstairs to the princess's salon. We stand and wait for another 15 minutes. The yellow and purple is much more evident here. Six large lavender chandeliers that look like candy floss adorn the ceiling. The salon is a suited to a teenage girl.

The princess steps out of her room.

The princess

SHE IS beautiful. She has the innocence of a little girl about her even though she has just celebrated her 27th birthday. She is wearing no make-up, only an eager smile. Her long black hair is pinned back with hair clips decorated with the word princess written in a gaudy pink.

She is elegant in casual sweats. Inviting me to sit, she exclaims with girlish delight, "Mrs C, you look so much younger than in your photos." So much for Photoshop. I tell her to call me Cay but she shakes her head and tells me that as I am older than her mother, she will call me "Mrs C" as a mark of respect. We are served fresh orange juice. She doesn't take her eyes off me. I give her the yoga DVD I got her as a gift and she looks at me as if buying her a gift is unheard of. At least she is still smiling.

I ask her what she would prefer me to call her – Amira, Princess or Your Highness – as my protocol list says any of the three. This princess has firm ideas. She likes the sound of "Your Highness" although "Princess" is acceptable as well.

She tells me that she found a very good yoga instructor in Riyadh and the "coach", as the princess calls her, comes three times a week. Does this mean my services as a yogi will no longer be required? I don't ask.

As my contract states, I am to be a companion and shoulder to cry on. She immediately begins to confide parts of her troubled intimate life that seem inappropriate for a first encounter. I detect a neediness that I'm not sure I can fill. She tells me of the many people who have wronged her. I can only listen.

My princess, although the second oldest, was the first of the children to marry so it was a lavish affair. Top international designers were flown in to Riyadh to take measurements and the Amira's favourite hairdresser was flown in from France.

After only four months, her husband, without the princess knowing it, uttered the three lines, "I divorce thee, I divorce thee, I divorce thee" – all it takes for a man to annul his marriage. The princess moved back home, this time to her own villa.

This was not an arranged marriage. Her ex-husband is a cousin and, according to her, turned out to be abusive.

Forced marriages happen to this day and females are not involved in making decisions about their own marriages. The marriage contract is between the husband-to-be and the father of the bride.

Polygyny is legal in Saudi Arabia. Saudi men may take as many as four wives, provided that they can support each of their wives equally. Women are allowed only one husband and cannot marry non-Muslim men unless they are granted official permission.

After the breakdown of her marriage, the princess retreated to her bed where she has been hiding out for five years. She rises only for regular weekly family dinners and for appointments with her psychiatrist three times a week. And sometimes – not always – for desert dinners.

She sits on her bed with three laptops around her and updates her four Facebook profiles daily. On one of the sites, she is a 21-year-old girl who likes champagne and partying. She spends most of her life on different forums in cyberspace as there is not much else for her to do.

After two hours, I'm dismissed. I head to the gate. There seems to be a lot of fussing as I stand to one side waiting for the driver. "Madam, is this your purse?" asks one of the drivers. He hands me my purse. Somehow, while searching for hand cream in my too-big bag on my way to the palace it must have fallen out and onto the back seat. The driver insists that I check the contents.

All the money I arrived with in Saudi earlier in the day is gone. I converted ten thousand rand into dollars only the previous day at the airport. The driver had only one passenger after dropping us, the royal hairdresser. She handed the purse to the driver – but clearly not before emptying it. In a land where you can get your hand chopped off for theft, I am at a loss for words.

Mona tells me that when the woman entered the palace, she was flustered and avoided eye contact, disappearing upstairs without greeting anyone. She added that there is just no way that the drivers would even be tempted to steal as their jobs mean too much to them. They support large families back home.

That night, lying in bed in the dark, I yearn for home and for contact with loved ones but I still don't have any means of communication.

The medical

❧

MY FIRST work day starts at four in the afternoon when most of the shops open for the day's trading. I am fetched at the gate by the driver who was on duty the night before. His name is Sultan.

My eyes are still bloodshot. The fine sand particles in the air cause this and it will be about a month before my eyes become used to it and clear completely.

I am introduced to the team of two Filipino and two Malawian girls I am to manage.

Mami is the housekeeper and outside cleaner. She is a rotund 56-year-old lady with a laugh that matches her girth. She is a married mother of four – two boys in their late teens and two girls in their early twenties. They live with Mami's younger sister on the outskirts of Lilongwe in Malawi. Her husband works on the mines in South Africa and although they are in contact telephonically, she has not seen him in 18 months. They are doing what they have to do to make sure all their children are able to attend university. The two older children are enrolled at the nursing campus of the University of Malawi in Lilongwe.

Mami's fellow Malawian, Maria, is the most reserved of the maids. She is responsible for general housekeeping, and though she is tiny, her size shouldn't fool you – she has the energy of 10 people. She is 28, soft-spoken and respectful. She seems to relish Mami's leading role in the basement, shadowing her every move.

Lilly, an intelligent 25-year-old Filipino woman is the princess's maid. She is responsible for handling all the princess's clothes, including washing it all by hand. Lilly is the only cleaner allowed to clean the princess's room. I am responsible for supervising this, and watching her work is a pleasure as she is meticulous.

The fourth member of my team is 35-year-old Sunny. She is Filipino and is a general cleaner, an endearing girl whose smile lights up a room. Her tiny frame hides formidable strength. She has the delightful habit of coming up behind me when I least expect it to give me a hug. I love her spontaneity as hugs are pretty scarce in Saudi.

Since her contract began, she has met a fellow Filipino online and their cyber-romance is now in its second year. Any contact with a man who is not a relative is forbidden while in the employ of the princess so this is done in utmost secrecy.

He lives and works in the States and they plan to marry once she gets out. I turn a blind eye as these girls have so little interaction with the outside world and they are young, after all. Sunny is chomping at the bit to get home, as her contract ended eight months ago but she is being held against her will.

Two of the girls in our villa are desperate to go home. Their contracts expired months ago, but the princess realises that once they leave, they will never return, despite any assurances, so she has decided that no one may leave until she finds replacements. To find servants she is happy with can take over a year.

The princess summons me. A majestic bed dominates her room. Purple drapes hang from the ceiling, framing the bed on each side. There are murals on all the exposed walls. Although large, the room is cluttered. Boxes of possessions, bought on the princess's most recent trip to Paris, fill each corner, still unopened.

After exaggerated pleasantries, she informs me that I will be fetched at seven that evening to have my medical for my

— 49 —

iqama. Every expat has to undergo this to cement a year's work visa as the original visa is valid only for three months.

She invites me to sit so we can become better acquainted. We talk for hours. She appears vulnerable – a victim of many wrongs. I listen, and readily express sympathy, which seems to make her even more forthcoming. For one so young, she is suspicious, mistrustful and very angry. But still I have no inkling of the cruel nature that lies behind her sweet smile.

The driver collects me promptly at seven. We are accompanied by a tiny old lady, wizened by the desert sun. She argues heatedly with the driver in Arabic, her voice a knife's edge. I am sitting in range of her vengeful spittle, which sprays everything within reach. I endure 40 minutes of this before we enter a filthy, rundown, heavily populated neighbourhood. Stray cats in various stages of malnutrition wander the littered streets. The sight depresses me no end.

Accompanied by the driver, I walk up a grimy flight of stairs to the clinic on the first floor. Every seat is taken, and the rundown room is crowded with patients, standing, waiting. The stillness is broken by coughing and a kid's screams from further down the passage. The smell of a rubbish dump hangs in the air. Torn posters hang off the pale green walls. At reception, the driver discusses the necessary, again in Arabic. My elbows stick to the counter.

I am ushered into a small, dank, poorly lit room where two medical personnel wrestle with a pile of files a foot high. The princess had given me two bottles beforehand so that I could deliver my samples in private, but no matter how hard I tried, I could only fill one. Handing me the empty bottle, the doctor insists I give him a stool sample. Though there has been no sign of any stools over the past five days, I now have to produce one on demand! I don't know whether to laugh or cry. The more I tell him that this is not possible, the more he insists. I trudge off to the bathroom.

What meets me fill me with disgust. My chest heaves involuntarily. The floor is wet with urine and streaks of faeces smear the walls. My stomach churns at the stench. This strengthens my resolve; with the hem of my abaya hitched knee high, I turn around, the bottle empty. I feel humiliated as I try to explain this to the doctor while the palace driver looks on. With no choice but to settle for the urine sample, the doctor turns his back on me. He scratches around noisily in a metal filing cabinet and takes out a single syringe. My eyes lock on his long dirty fingernails. He draws blood without wearing gloves. I sit there, inert with disbelief.

Next up are chest X-rays. This time a woman calls my name. Relieved to be done with the abrupt stool doctor, I follow her orders and disrobe. She walks over to me and roughly shoves my shoulders closer to the X-ray machine. She is impatient, and seems terribly annoyed with the world. So much for the softer touch.

The driver and I walk two blocks down the road to where the car is parked. Men mill about outside, chatting in groups. The traffic noise off the street is deafening, it is not a beautiful noise. The hot evening air, thick with exhaust fumes, feels suffocating. Everyone stares. Even wearing the hijab, I clearly stand out as a foreigner. I feel dirty and violated. A lump is forming in my throat.

As we settle back into the car, the old woman picks up where she left off. This time the driver reciprocates. Their loud angry outburst sets me off. My throat constricts as my stoicism crumbles and tears run freely down my face. The old lady is so involved in what she is trying to get across to the driver that she doesn't notice. The misery reflected back to me from the city streets doesn't help.

Back at the compound, I drop all my clothes on the floor, flinging the abaya into the furthest corner of the bathroom, and drain the geyser of hot water. God, what I would give for a glass of wine. I fall into an exhausted sleep.

In the morning, I still feel traumatised. Mona and I discuss my experience at breakfast. She says I was brave to have held out until I got to the car. She had not had a predelivered sample, and was forced to use the toilet at the clinic. She had burst into tears right there. The acrid reek of urine soaked into the hem of her abaya followed her home. She stopped crying only when she stood underneath the pelting heat of the shower.

Second day at work

I START at two in the afternoon on my second day so I have ample time to get myself positively psyched for the day ahead and put last night to the back of my mind. The dragging tiredness has abated somewhat although my eyes remain bloodshot.

As I arrive at the palace, I leave my shoes at the door. As from today, I am to walk around the villa in socks. It is a comfortable arrangement and as the floors are spotless, I happily oblige. I spend the day summing up what has to be done, making lists and getting to know where everything is.

The princess calls. She expresses concern about my red eyes and hands me a gel to alleviate dry eyes. The thick liquid instantly dissolves mascara. I am looking at her through a haze, as if I'd opened my eyes underwater.

Nine hours later I thank God for the sock arrangement. There are a lot of stairs to climb, numerous times a day. The laundry on the top floor is outside on the roof so that noise is kept to a minimum. It is a sleek, modern room with rows and rows of well organised shelves.

Tomorrow I plan to get better acquainted with the staff but I spend time working with each of them today, asking questions and making notes. They all have their duties, defined long before my arrival so I listen, while I observe their presentation. They are extremely polite and respectful. The two Filipinos are more reserved than the Malawian women who chatter cheerfully. When everyone is present in the basement kitchen, the focal point, the rule is that only English is permitted to be spoken. Surprisingly everyone sticks to this rule, which I'm grateful for.

I am called up again. I knock softly and the princess asks me in. I sit with her for two hours taking notes on how she wants things done. Her list of demands gives me a little more insight into her troubled character. She is a germaphobe. Every inch of her villa is cleaned every day. This includes the windows, even though her curtains are always drawn. As we walk around, I write as fast as I can. All door handles have to be wiped after anyone from the outside has entered the villa, and that applies to family too.

We proceed to her bathroom. It is the size of my entire cottage at home. She points to the bidet. "I don't know about you people but we use the bidet every time we go." I smile slightly at her comment but I don't respond.

— 55 —

The conversation then takes a nasty turn as the princess abruptly changes the subject. "Under no circumstances trust the maids. They come from conditions where they live worse than animals! They are no better than animals!" she says contemptuously. Her face distorts as she leaves the statement hanging, to maximise its malicious impact. She looks at me with raised eyebrows, waiting for me to agree. I have no choice but to reply, "Yes, Your Highness." It is protocol.

I feel as if I have betrayed myself.

At eleven, the princess tells me I may leave. After throwing the abaya over my head and putting on my shoes, I feel for the plastic container of pellets in my handbag. I had asked Sultan to buy me a bag when he went shopping.

As I walk to the gate, the pitiful meowing from the bushes becomes louder. I prise the lid off the container. With a flick of my wrist, hoping no one from the main palace is looking out at just that moment; I throw the pellets in the direction of the noise and quickly return the container to my handbag. The meowing stops immediately.

Buying laptops and cell phones

❦

MONA IS instructed by my princess to take me shopping for a new cell phone and a laptop – at my own expense. I have not received my iqama yet so I have to buy what I need on Mona's iqama.

On our way to work, we stop at a popular book store where you can buy pretty much anything electronic. The sales men standing around talking to one another behind the counter ignore me. I am the only person at the counter, but I am evidently invisible. I don't interrupt them. I notice a young man, no older than 18, with a store badge pinned to his shirt, standing alone to the side. I ask for his help. He looks around in a panic.

He is a trainee so he calls a colleague for help – one of the men behind the counter. He walks over to us, scowling, highly irritated at being disturbed, especially to assist a woman. He is abrupt and refuses to make eye contact. I will be spending thousands of riyals but that seems irrelevant.

I am still bristling at the way women are treated – I haven't been here long enough to have become accustomed to it. Note to self: rein that in!

We are third in our queue when the second call for prayer comes. The cashiers drop everything and walk away. For the love of God! This means a 30-minute wait until prayer time is over. I don't know whether I can bear to stand in one spot for half an hour but I have no choice. I wait.

Once back at the compound, I call home on my new mobile phone. Though I'm overjoyed to hear the voices of loved ones, the conversation is cryptic. Mona has warned me that our conversations, emails and text messages could be intercepted by the palace.

Contact with home takes on particular significance because I am in a potentially dangerous situation, so far away. It is comforting to know that I can speak to my loved ones within seconds. What did expats do in the past? Send smoke signals?

Day three

❧

SETTLING IN during the first week is challenging. I blow two electric sockets because the plug of my hairdryer is too loose. I use Mona's hairdryer, but it's obvious that she doesn't like it. Most of the instructions on my new laptop are in Arabic. My new mobile phone is much more difficult to operate than the simple one I have at home – and much of these instructions are in Arabic too. Trying to figure out everything is time consuming and fraught with frustration.

I am at work at two in the afternoon on day three. I start my first inventory in the kitchens as foodstuffs are perishable – the linen can wait. There are kitchens on four of the five floors of the villa, the main one in the basement where most of the princess's food is prepared. On the first floor – the entrance level – a designer kitchen contains every up-to-date appliance you can imagine, though most of these are still in boxes. This kitchen is untouched. It awaits a husband.

In all the kitchens, the cupboards are brimming with groceries bought on the royals' most recent trip to Paris. Twice a year they travel to France and Italy to shop for groceries and other luxuries. During these trips, our job entails boxing everything to send back to Saudi. I listen to Mona's stories of the last trip to Paris and, frankly, it sounds like a nightmare.

The previous year, the Filipino servants were taken along. But that was the last time, as the royals fear that they could escape to their embassy, to be sent home. All the work now falls on the butlers and PAs. They are on standby 24 hours a day, covering everything from hand washing clothing right down to cleaning toilets because hotel staff are not allowed over the threshold to the royals' rooms. So much for the romance of Paris.

On a previous trip, Mona had a free moment at the pool while the royals were out for the day. She ordered a glass of wine, for her own account, but there was a mistake with the billing. When Princess Arabella found that it had been added to the royals' account, she shouted at her in front of her own and the hotel staff in the reception hall. "You are disrespectful and a disgrace!" Mona retreated to her room in tears.

I rope in the two women I think will be best suited to helping with the inventory and we tackle the first cupboard. This takes me on a culinary trip of foodstuffs I never knew existed.

It is an efficient operation; one of the women unpacks the shelves and calls out the dates, the other cleans and I document and categorise.

I fill 18 boxes with expired goods from the last couple of months. I am appalled at the waste. The women tell me that serving a food item that has expired, even by one day, brings on a wrath in the princess that I have yet to experience. The following month will see further boxes filled, as will the month thereafter. Tins and jars of sauces, pestos and curry mixes – it is not so much the variety that is fascinating, but the quantity for one person.

The basement kitchen has 34 large cupboards so the kitchen inventory will take a whole week to complete.

After that, I'll make my way through five large boxes stacked in the lounge area in the basement. These contain expired French cosmetics – eye creams, skin toners and moisturisers dating back six years. And not just one of each – I count 29 bottles of toners. The same goes for the creams and lotions. The two last boxes are filled with expired medications – boxes and bottles of pills in every form for any ailment imaginable. Lilly, who is in charge of replenishing the cosmetics and medications, points out what each is used for. At least half the medication is for the treatment of depression.

The princess calls me up to her room. I have to wear a uniform, so she shows me several designs she has stored on her flash drive, each uglier than the one before. I eventually choose one, only for her to change it to something she prefers. I just go with the design she favours, consoling myself with the thought that no one will see me anyway.

I will have six uniforms, one for each work day. She chooses awful colour schemes, mixing colours that really don't belong together. The khaki with olive green resembles the colours worn by prisoners at home; I dub the navy blue and maroon combination my nurse's uniform. It is out of my hands.

Mona pops into our villa in the early evening. I am glad to see her. She is about to go upstairs to the princess's quarters, when I ask her to give me a minute – the princess has instructed me to announce the arrival of any visitors.

Mona is incensed but doesn't show it yet.

The same evening, an elderly Indian man comes to take my measurements. The princess speaks to him at length in Arabic, smiling often. She is in a jovial mood and the presence of the tailor seems to enhance this. Eventually she returns to her room.

The tailor shows me how to stand, legs apart and arms spread, in line with my shoulders. When he measures from my waist down to my crotch, I am shocked as his hand lingers too long while he writes down the measurements with his other hand. This is repeated at the back. Then he indicates that I should open my legs wider by slapping both of my inner thighs. He lodges his hand firmly between my legs and draws the tape measure down to my ankles.

Am I mistaken in thinking he is out of line? As he measures across my chest, there is no doubt about it – this tailor is too thorough. Why does his hand rest on my breast? I don't know how many lashes or years in jail I could get for slapping a man albeit an Indian man, not highly regarded by locals – so I resist. The experience leaves me pretty irritated.

I push his hand off and scowl at him. He backs off and this gives me the opportunity to call Lilly. He doesn't speak English, so I tell her to ask him if he has finished.

After I explain what has happened, Lilly is as annoyed as I am. The others have had the same experience.

On my way to the gate that evening, I look around to make sure no one is around before I remove the container from my bag and fling the pellets into the bushes.

Feeding the palace cats is risky, but later, during my second month there, the problem is solved.

Eli, the palace gatekeeper, lives in a tiny room right next to the gate. The drivers congregate here while waiting for their orders. I have such a soft spot for Eli but he is unaware of this.

I notice that the palace cats look healthier, and that they often hang around Eli's room. Late one evening, I announce my presence at Eli's door as he is sometimes required to phone the drivers to summon them from their accommodation when we are ready to be taken home. I spot one of the wild cats lying on Eli's bed.

On the way home, Sultan tells me that Eli shares his dinner with the cats. He never leaves the small room at the gate, and never has a day off, so I imagine that befriending the cats alleviates an otherwise very lonely existence. I ask Sultan to stop at the shop, so that I can buy a big bag of pellets to give to Eli. He might be the catalyst but I intend to make it as easy for him as I can.

As we arrive at the palace the following afternoon, I ask Sultan to stop at the gate for two seconds. I jump out of the car as quickly as I can, hiding the bag of pellets in the voluminous folds of my abaya. When I hand Eli the cat food wrapped in several bags to hide its contents, he frowns.

Curtly, in broken English, he tells me that he cannot keep it in his room. I nod, and immediately get back into the car.

Sultan explains that Eli's room is searched from time to time. He doesn't say this but I understand that getting caught feeding the cats will lead to a beating.

Every night from then on, I hand Eli the plastic container with just enough pellets for one meal for all the cats. Whenever there are too many drivers around, I give the bowl to Sultan, who passes it on to Eli. It is a happy arrangement, a conspiracy that forges a friendly bond between the three of us. With Eli, though, it doesn't go beyond the knowing looks of kindred souls.

Back at the compound, at the end of the third day, music is blaring from the poolside. The mood is happy.

Mona is home. She states (in capital letters) that there was no need for me to announce her arrival at the villa – she comes and goes freely. "I am just following protocol," I respond. Her nose is out of joint but at this early stage I don't know how to fix it. She continues to sulk at the perceived affront, so I say goodnight early just to get away from her. My closed bedroom door allows no further conversation.

I try to fall asleep but the noise coming from Mona's room is deafening. Our headboards are head to head on each side of the plasterboard wall and Mona snores like a Massey Ferguson. Sleep takes a long time to come.

The next morning, when I come back from the pool, Mona is sitting in the kitchen with a cup of coffee. The greeting is strained. I rearrange my bedroom so that my headboard is against the opposite wall. I don't think this will help much but after a couple of sleepless nights, I am willing to try anything.

First visit to Tamimi's

❧

TODAY I am going grocery shopping for the first time. Tamimi stores are everywhere. Sultan finds a shady spot under an awning and even before I am out of the car, he is already moving his seat back. It's an opportunity for him to catch some shut eye. The drivers survive on these brief naps.

As there is no rush, I take my time walking through the aisles. They are spacious and well marked, filled with black cloaked figures moving slowly, sedately around. I blend in well. The Saudi women shoppers I approach for directions are helpful and gracious.

I am blown away by the variety but even more so by the prices. Compared to home, everything is so inexpensive. A can of Coke, not the silly airline ones, is about a third of the price at home. There is a staggering choice of yoghurt, also a fraction of the price I expect. I stand in awe at the confectionery counter.

The fresh produce section is chilled and the fruit and vegetables look fresh and appetising.

I walk past the magazine section and stand for a moment to take it all in. On all the magazines, exposed parts of the body, like arms, have been blacked out. Many people wonder how this happens, It's a well-kept secret, but I have heard, and believe, that the covert "Black Hand" society is responsible.

Armed with black marker pens, the Black Hand vowed to erase all haraam pictures from the land. They formed squads that roam the streets at night, entering warehouses, post offices, and malls. The Black Hand has duplicate keys to any building they need to enter. These are obtained by force, or provided by their members.

The Black Hand members carry small rucksacks, containing extra markers, and all photos of anything construed as haraam, are blacked out. Some members even black out words like "pork".

They work hard, but sometimes miss an arm or a leg. Previously, punishments for these omissions were severe. Miss a whole woman or a pig? A finger was chopped off. Miss a woman in lingerie? That's your hand. Miss a naked woman? Chop! There goes that male member!

Friday off

❧

AFTER A week of intense duties, I am so looking forward to our first Friday off. Mona suggests we take a taxi to some of the ultra-modern malls. As she has been here months longer, I let her take charge – and it's a role she seems to relish.

Three of us, Mona, myself and a fellow South African ex-pat, Tracy, squeeze into the taxi. The cluttered interior makes me laugh. You need to keep your elbows and knees in to avoid dislodging the bags of miniature chocolates hanging off the front seats, the eight boxes of strategically placed tissues or the fake flowers that adorn the roof.

We arrive at the mall during prayer time so all the stores are closed.

One designer shop follows another. After walking around for about 30 minutes, I feel deflated and down. I have never been much of a shopper – I find it somehow lonely and a little pathetic. Walking from one closed shop window to another, on the only day we get off in a week, is not my idea of recreation.

We end our excursion with a coffee at Starbucks, in the family section.

Though there are many restaurants and hundreds of coffee shops in the city, I can't even go for a coffee. A woman who enters a restaurant alone is seen as immoral and could be chased out like a stray dog.

Segregation is particularly strict in restaurants, as eating requires removal of the veil. Most restaurants in Saudi Arabia have "family" and "bachelor" sections. In the family section, diners are usually seated in separate rooms or behind screens and curtains.

Waiters are expected to allow women time to cover up before they enter, although they don't always stick to this practice. The mutawa particularly favour restaurants. They go from table to table, inspecting the iqamas of the diners. Valentine's Day is one of the most fruitful days for arrests.

Sexual segregation, which keeps wives, sisters and daughters from contact with male strangers, follows from concern for female purity and family honour. At social events, men and women don't usually mix.

Most Saudi homes have one entrance for men and another for women. If a male who is not a relative enters the female section of a Saudi home, this is a violation of family honour. This section is "haram" which means "forbidden" and "sacred".

Private space is associated with women while public space, like the living room, is reserved for men. Traditional house designs incorporate high walls, compartmentalised inner rooms, and curtains to protect women.

As public life is very much the domain of men, women are expected to veil themselves outside their homes. Although Sharia laws are not applied as strictly to expats, I keep my head covered with a hijab when I'm out, or risk a public chastising. If you're seen without it, the mutawa storm over, telling you, loudly and aggressively, to cover up. Blondes especially are targeted, and subjected to regular confrontations.

Public transport is segregated, as are beaches and amusement parks, so some have different hours for men and women. "Khalwa" is the term for violation of the principles of sexual segregation.

I learn a little about these rules when I open a bank account. As I walk in, I stand at the back of the only queue, of 34 men, as I know no better. I ignore the stares – I am becoming slightly immune to them. These men are mostly expats sending their wages home.

A bank official walks over to me and kindly tells me that

I am in the wrong queue. He directs me to the non-existent women's queue. I now understand the stares. I am served immediately. I can't help feeling a little smug as sexual segregation has worked in my favour for once. I am out of the bank in 15 minutes. As I leave, I glance over my shoulder. The men's queue has hardly moved.

We arrive back at the compound after my first off day and I feel sad. I miss home. I work to the best of my ability but I also need down-time to function properly. It seems to be all work and no play so far.

Cats

❦

MY IMPRESSION of Saudi Arabia is of a land of rich sheikhs who live lavishly in extravagant palaces, their unbelievable riches stemming from the black gold.

This may be true for a minority of Saudis, but I soon see another side to the coin, and it's not all that shiny. Poverty, unemployment, hunger, beggars, shack villages – these all exist in Saudi Arabia.

Some Saudis live in mud houses, often without running water, plumbing or electricity. The goatherds build straw huts. And others have no option but to live in shacks or even on the streets. Their struggles are unseen; they're the forgotten ones, the "dirty" secrets. Many of them are widowed or divorced women with no source of income, no way to find work, no way to get to work.

I can't quite reconcile this with the great emphasis Islam places on zakat – charity to the poor. Many Saudis give zakat during Ramadan only, when, it is believed, blessings are multiplied.

I cannot help but notice the many cats sitting around the rubbish bins all over Riyadh. One of the places they congregate is on an open piece of ground where the bins are, just a hundred metres from the gate of our compound. It distresses me that these cats aren't pets; they're seen as pests. They are in a terrible condition, and so thin. Every time I see them – every day – I feel a pain that is physical.

On the way home one evening, I ask Sultan to stop at a Tamimi's for a bag of cat pellets once again. He laughs and shakes his head as he is not too fond of them either.

I pour some pellets into a plastic bowl. As I walk over to the open ground, I shake the plastic container and call out to them. At least 10 pairs of eyes watch me as I make little piles of pellets spaced about two metres apart.

The cats come running from all directions but clearly, even in the cat world, there is a hierarchy – fur flies as they fight for the food. I favour the kittens and chase the bigger cats away so that they have a chance. A grey kitten about two months old rubs up against me but when I try to pet him, he runs away. I pour out a little heap just for him and stand guard as he eats. These cats are so hungry that they seem to swallow the pellets whole.

I hear a terrible noise, a high pitched whine, from underneath one of the cars parked nearby. I go down on my knees to find a ginger cat with a newborn kitten whose eyes aren't open yet. It rips at my heart, seeing her trying to protect her kitten. How can she produce milk when she is starving? Where is the rest of her litter? She does not allow me to get close to her but I scrape up some of the pellets that haven't been eaten yet and gently throw them towards her. She is so spooked by my presence that I step back, hoping that she gets to eat.

I walk home with a heavy heart as there are just too many of them. God knows, feeding them is only alleviating their suffering temporarily. I almost trip over the grey kitten playfully running in and out from underneath my abaya. Still, he does not allow me to touch him. He walks me right to the compound door.

Meeting Serge

❦

IT'S FRIDAY. Although the Holy Day in KSA, it is a day that promises bliss for the sheer fact that we have the day off to do whatever we like.

The previous evening, our neighbours, two Lebanese medics, invited us to meet up with them and some of the other expats in the afternoon. After several invitations to join them over the past while, this is the first Friday Mona and I are able to do so.

There are 12 people sitting around the pool, who are mostly Lebanese. Our fellow expats from the compound are already in a party mood as homemade arak and red wine has done the rounds.

Arak is Lebanon's most popular alcoholic drink after beer and wine. Clear in its pure form but milky when mixed with water, it has the smooth, refreshing taste of liquorice. If you like liquorice, that is.

Conversation comes easily as everyone has questions. They want to know where we're from and what brought us here.

— 76 —

They are exceptionally well mannered and gallant. Every now and again, a guy I would get to know as Neo picks up his tribal drum set. As he starts singing, everyone falls in, clapping with unadulterated enthusiasm. We are delighted by their easy camaraderie.

One man in particular stands out, because he chooses not to stand out. We are briefly introduced but with all the names presented, his name escapes me.

He confidently leans back in his chair with his legs crossed, watching and listening. His arm is casually draped across his lap. The hand stroking a crystal rosary is practiced and relaxed, playing it like a finely stringed instrument. I watch his hand when I think he won't notice.

My blonde friend Lea is visiting us today. She's in her bikini. The guys, with the exception of the man with the rosary who is sticking by my side, fight for the seat next to her. It is quite amusing to watch.

There seems to be no age discrimination among the expat men; young guys in their twenties flirt with me. I have nephews a decade older, for goodness sake. There are just not enough women to go around so whenever a new girl appears on the scene, the guys jostle for position.

Mark, a twenty-eight-year-old British expat who is an English lecturer at a university in Riyadh tells me of an upcoming event, Christmas carols in the desert, organised by the Hash Club. As luck would have it, the event falls on my birthday which is also on a Friday. He invites me to join him and some colleagues on the day. I am ecstatic.

The conversation turns to books and *Fifty shades of Grey* is mentioned by Lea. "That book is hot!" She exclaims. I add that I've heard that apparently it resembles a Mills & Boon, the only difference being that it contains hard-core porn. I am told that I am not really allowed an opinion until I have read the book. Mark has it on his Kindle, and offers to loan it to me.

I chat to several people over the course of the afternoon, but I am constantly aware of the man with the rosary. As yet, I am totally unaware of my attraction to him.

As late afternoon turns to early evening, everyone now best friends, we laugh uproariously. The aroma of shisha pipes fills the warm air. I ask if I may try one. They all watch in anticipation as I blow the air out of my lungs before I inhale. The liquid gurgles at my effort yet I manage to only take in a small amount of the aromatic strawberry-tinged smoke. I feel giddy, which makes everyone laugh. The cameraderie is enhanced by the prevailing attitude – what happens in the compound stays in the compound. And now Mona and I are part of the pack.

Deeper into the evening, he sits quietly amid the singing and spurts of traditional Lebanese dancing. His head tilted back, a slight smile around his sensuous mouth, he holds my gaze a little too long. I feel a shift that takes place when the chemistry kicks in and for a moment it leaves me breathless.

I say goodnight earlier than most. He is the only one who stands up when I get up to leave. Just before I walk away, I ask him his name again. "My name is Serge," he says with a smile.

Heading out with the princess

❧

I AM informed by the princess that I will be accompanying her to a doctor's appointment today, the first occasion I have to play by the protocol rules outside the palace grounds. I fetch her abaya and hijab from the laundry and Milly drowns the garment in perfume. We leave the villa, the princess shrouded in black, and wearing the biggest sunglasses I have ever seen. I walk two paces behind her.

Driver ready, check. Water in the car, check. Sultan, my princess's personal driver is waiting with the back right hand door open. He stands with his back to us because eye contact with the princess is forbidden, unless she speaks to him directly. The princess is tense and I feel it spill over to me, tightening the knot in my stomach.

As she is seated, Sultan closes her door and only then do I walk round to the other side to slide in beside her. I notice the rear view mirror is turned up to the ceiling as even an accidental glance in the princess's direction will bring the wrath of God upon him.

— 80 —

Is this the same man who drives us home at night, often at 160km an hour, the man we have to beg to slow down? He is the model of decorum, sitting so upright, his head almost touching the ceiling.

On our way to work one day, the Amir phones. Sultan immediately snaps his fingers which means total silence from the back seat. Sultan speaks in tones reserved exclusively for the Amir. His voice becomes soft and melodious, and he ends each sentence with Masha Allah or Al Hamdu Lilah. He even appears to be sitting up straighter. I hear our names, madam Cay and madam Mona, mentioned.

The drivers, generally from Sudan and Egypt, each carry three mobile phones. The first is kept only for the Amir, the second, for general work duties, contact by the palace staff and switchboard, and the third, for personal use. Each royal has their own driver and own car but the Amir has the right to all the drivers.

Once he is off the phone, Sultan starts to panic. The Amir wants him to fetch his Porsche from the garage 50 metres away from the palace doors and have it parked outside in 15 minutes. We are stuck in traffic. Twenty minutes later we have hardly made progress. The Amir phones again, and we can hear him shouting. In a soft voice, Sultan assures him that we are on our way. The drivers are terrified of the Amir because they have received many a beating. Mona has seen it happen.

As we leave the palace grounds one day, Sultan stops abruptly, sending my laptop flying onto the floor. He jumps out of the car and runs to pick up an empty Starbucks cup lying on the grass strip surrounding the palace. Mona explains that if the Amir sees rubbish anywhere near the palace, he whips the drivers. The reason for Sultan's haste is that the Amir is just behind us.

For this particular outing with the princess, the drive is smooth, with no cutting in and out of traffic.

As Mona has warned me never to make conversation with the princess while travelling, unless she speaks to me first, I make a concerted effort to stare out of the window. It doesn't lessen the tension in the car.

Most of the signage at our destination is in Arabic but I spot the word "psychiatrist". Sultan jumps from the car and opens the princess's door. I climb out unaided. She seems intent on getting inside even though no one could possibly recognise her with those oversized sunglasses and the hijab covering her head and the lower part of her face.

I walk a pace behind her but as we reach the first door, I speed up to pass her and open the door. This first attempt is a bit clumsy as I pull instead of push but by the time we reach the second door, I have it down pat. I am surprised to see the reception staff in black from head to toe. As with the few other women in the workplace, they work with their abayas on and their faces covered.

Traditionally, companies that hire women have created all-female areas. Western companies – like McDonald's, Pizza Hut and Starbucks – enforce Saudi religious regulations in restaurants, prompting comparisons to apartheid among Western activists. The facilities in the family sections are usually inferior.

The number of mixed-gender workplaces has increased since King Abdullah was crowned, although they are still unusual. Even then, the women have to wear the full black regalia. The only exceptions to the rules are seen at some hospitals, medical colleges, and banks.

The princess is ushered in and I take a seat in the now empty waiting room. A huge TV attached to the wall shows throngs of pilgrims at Mecca, walking anti-clockwise around the Kaaba, Islam's holiest shrine located in the grand mosque at the heart of the city, while prayers are repeated on an endless loop.

I have brought along Mark's kindle and quickly pick up

where I left off. I am in the middle of *Fifty Shades of Grey* – since he had said I should read it before giving my opinion. I find it painful. It really is like a Mills & Boon, just with porn. As bodies writhe in pleasure on the pages of my book, I guiltily look up as another woman enters the waiting room and the images of Mecca stare down at me again.

Three hours later the princess emerges just as the characters in the book enter the infamous Red Room. The princess seems in a much better frame of mind and the door opening goes off smoothly as we make our way back down to the car.

She is chatty on our return journey, pointing out certain buildings of interest.

We pass a hospital. "That is a beauty hospital with very good doctors," the Princess remarks. "I will send you there for Botox." She looks at me as if she has just shared the news that I had won the lottery. Biting my tongue has become routine – I don't say a word, though it may just be that her comment renders me speechless. Am I really in such need of Botox?

By the time we get back to the villa, most of the daily chores have been done. On the spur of the moment, I decide to bake cupcakes. The mix is already rich, but I add chocolate chips and a handful of crushed walnuts. I am surprised at how well they turn out. I am having so much fun; I swirl thick chocolate icing onto the cakes and top them off with the bright pink flowers the princess has in her cupboard. They look beautiful.

The staff gather in the kitchen to admire my handiwork. I ask Sunny to go upstairs to get one of the princess's plates and to set a tray for me. She happily obliges, no doubt anticipating a cupcake.

I put on rubber gloves and take the tray upstairs. Two cupcakes adorn the plate.

After knocking, I walk in with the tray. The princess's face lights up. She sits for a moment without saying anything while she admires the cakes. "Mrs C, thank you so much!" she gushes.

It is only eight but the princess tells me I may go. It almost seems as if she is rewarding me for baking. As good as the day was, I need no excuse to gather my things and hotfoot it out of there.

On our way home, I get a text message, "Hello Mrs C, the cupcakes r soooo delicious! Thx a looot 4 baking them 4 me! U really made my day J Thx 4 taking care of me... Nite nite & c u 2mrw INSHA ALLAH xoxo"

Right now, sitting in that dark car, speeding through the streets of Riyadh, I couldn't be happier.

There is a saying that comes to mind soon after; just when you think you have everything under control, God laughs...

First visit to Doctor Friendly

❧

HALF AN hour later, we draw up outside the compound. The drivers have been instructed to wait until we are inside before pulling away. I am almost at the gate when a searing pain shoots up my ankle. I double over, dropping everything I am carrying.

Sultan has seen what has happened and is next to me in an instant. He goes down on one knee and lifts my foot. Any other time, his look of alarm would have been funny. My sandal is nailed to my foot by a screw, most of its length embedded in my heel. I try to dislodge my sandal but the pain is severe and the nail doesn't budge.

I sink onto the grass beside the paved concrete. Even in this state, I cannot help noticing the many cats that take refuge under parked cars. They sit and watch us.

Sultan, bless him, keeps talking, gently, soothingly, in Arabic, as he firmly grips my sandal and pulls it away from my foot. I didn't anticipate that, and my guttural scream frightens me as much as it does him. For a moment I sit there, eyes

— 86 —

closed, trying to catch my breath. I am surprised at the amount of blood that is gushing from the hole.

I thank him and after assuring him that I am okay, he helps me up. I limp to our flat, leaving a bloody trail on the terracotta tiles in the compound. I have the rusty nail with me, and realise I will have to go for a tetanus shot as the last one I had was as a child. I clean the wound as best I can and wrap it up firmly, more to staunch the flow of blood than anything else.

I will go to hospital first thing in the morning.

When I wake up, my heel is swollen out of shape. I phone the princess and after I explain what has happened, she sends Sultan for me straight away. An hour later, I am sitting in the waiting room at the hospital. Although medical aid is part of my contract, it doesn't quite work that way. The princess pays all the medical bills so you aren't free to go to a doctor without her knowing. Unless you pay for it yourself.

This is the family doctor and also a personal friend of the royals, even travelling with them on their trips to Europe. He is not available immediately as it is prayer time. I can't help wondering what would happen if a patient was at death's door at prayer time. Insha'Allah I won't find out. I've become used to waiting, so I don't go anywhere without something to read. I take out Mark's kindle and settle in.

Doctor "Friendly" is standing in front of me with a smile and his hand extended. I get up, but jerk backwards forcefully, the neckline of my abaya under my chin. I had stepped on the hem at the back as I got up. He waits with his hand extended and this time I manage the second attempt at standing with a little more dignity.

He asks where I'm from, then responds by greeting me with, "*Goeie môre. Hoe gaan dit?*" accompanied by a beaming smile. Sometime in his life he had dated a South African and takes great pride in the few Afrikaans words he can still speak. He is very talkative and asks me many questions. "How are you enjoying Riyadh?" "How is work going?" "Do you like working for the princess?"

I did not know that the princess had confided to Mona that Dr Friendly is in love with her. Had she mentioned that, I would have been very wary about what I told him. For this reason, my second visit to him is the beginning of the end . . .

After the tetanus injection, Sultan is waiting for me, as always. This time he jumps out and opens the door back for me, a courtesy usually reserved for the princess.

As I limp into the villa, Lilly says the princess is waiting to see me. I knock and she beckons me in. I try not to limp as I walk in but the friendly doc did not give me painkillers. This calls for two myprodols and a shot of whisky but neither is at hand. In this topsy-turvy world, antibiotics are available over the counter but any medication that will make you look at your neighbour twice, is banned. So are pool noodles and anything else deemed phallic.

The princess is concerned but I assure her I am all right. I am still new on the job and don't want to give the impression that I'm a hypochondriac, so after the pleasantries, I pull the four centimetre nail out of my pocket to show the princess the culprit. She shrieks as she whips back as if an invisible force had just backhanded her. Apparently she doesn't have a strong stomach. Imagine I had shown her the gaping hole in my foot! I limp out backwards.

A shopping spree with Lilly

TODAY LILLY is taking me shopping for our villa, to show me the ropes. Although most of our groceries come from the main palace, there are certain items the princess buys that the palace does not. We also need to buy perfume. Who buys 20 bottles of perfume at once? When I see that it lasts about a month, I understand.

Lilly and Sultan chat in Arabic. They seem to have a good relationship, bordering on flirtatious. I think back to another snippet of information imparted by Mona – that the two of them are having an affair. How in God's name is this possible? But whatever there is between them, good for them. Lilly's life is miserable enough; if she finds anything that will make her life a little easier after two years and nine months, she is welcome to it. The princess has, however, instructed me to not let her out of my sight.

We arrive at the mall as prayer time starts. Sultan drops us off as he goes off to prayers too. We walk up and down, looking into the closed shops. I turn to speak to Lilly; she is not there.

I stand in one spot, scanning the crowd – mostly women

waiting for the supermarket to open its grid door. It is difficult to spot Lilly in a sea of black. Everyone looks the same in their abayas and as Lilly is a devout Muslim, she wears the head scarf as well, so trying to pick her out is even more difficult. I try to phone her but she does not hear her phone.

About 10 minutes later, as the grid slides up, Lilly appears beside me. I am a little harsher with her than I intend to be but I am responsible for her when we are out, so she should know better than to put me in a situation like this. She takes it in her stride – just smiles and says, "Yes, Madam."

Up to now I have only been inside a Tamimi's, so I find the rows and rows of imported goods fascinating. Lilly is a font of information on items I haven't seen before. The prices again surprise me – everything is so inexpensive. This is home, 20 years ago. It takes about an hour to get everything on the list. Finally, I slip a bag of cat pellets into the trolley – for my own account, of course.

We are now into the second prayer time for the afternoon. Although shoppers are locked in during prayer time and can continue to do their shopping, there are no tellers. All the staff are on their knees in the fresh produce section, facing Mecca. But in between Mecca and where they are kneeling is a ceiling to floor fridge unit packed with meat and advertising lamb at today's specials in huge neon letters.

Prayer times

๛

Salat al-fajr:	dawn, before sunrise
Salat al-zuhr:	midday, after the sun passes its highest point
Salat al-'asr:	the late part of the afternoon
Salat al-maghrib:	just after sunset
Salat al-'isha:	between sunset and midnight

ONE OF the more challenging aspects of adapting to life in Saudi Arabia is getting used to the working hours and days off. Many businesses work split days, and the prayer ritual is repeated five times a day by millions of people around the world.

Even shopping malls operate on split hours, so shops are closed for several hours during an afternoon. In fact, all shops, businesses and restaurants close four times a day for 30 minutes for prayer – most are not open at the time of the first prayer, which is why there are typically four closures rather than five. As a result, you try to run errands between prayers, hoping you don't get caught with your errand unfinished at prayer time. Many a time, I stood outside a store waiting for them to reopen.

Before 2013, the official weekend days were Thursday and Friday. However, Saudi was shut down for two days while businesses and financial markets in the rest of the world remained active. History was made in April of that year, when the Saudi weekend was changed to Friday and Saturday.

Back at the palace, I leave the girls to unpack as the princess is calling for me. She is furious. In our absence, Sunny served the princess her usual morning fruit and yoghurt but the yoghurt had expired that day. I make sure the fridges are checked daily but our excursion to the mall meant we had not yet done this.

I am learning that when the princess is on the rampage, it is best to stand still and say nothing but "Yes, Your Highness".

"What are the staff doing?" she yells. "I will not eat old food!" I know that she does not want an answer; she needs to vent. "You must punish them, Mrs C!" I ask her what punishment she has in mind. "We are going to Europe soon; make them clean all my suitcases." That seems reasonable so I excuse myself and help the girls as they start dismantling the towering pile of 36 large suitcases taking up half the living area in the basement.

The maids' quarters are in the basement, two to a spacious room, each with its own bathroom. The maids may not leave the villa even to dump the rubbish without the princess's permission. During my time there, two of them never left the premises – not once. They endure two years of this and in most cases they are kept long after their two-year contracts are up.

Cleaning the suitcases turns into a fun experience as everyone climbs in. I cut off all the old labels, Sunny, the culprit, soaks off the remnants of the stickers stuck to the cases in a solution of warm soapy water. Lilly wipes them on the inside and Maria, on the outside. Two hours later the cases are clean and back in place. Everyone feels a sense of accomplishment as we put the kettle on for tea.

I go up to the princess's room. As she has calmed down by now, I ask her if she would like something to drink. We have a kind of game going on; whenever I make her tea, I surprise her with a flavour I have chosen from her "tea cupboard", which must hold over a hundred different teas from different countries. Some are for stress, others for relaxation, for sleep, to wake up, to induce an appetite, to reduce appetite, for premenstrual tension, for bloating – the list is endless.

There is a collection of mugs in her upstairs kitchen, some with the word "princess" written on them in different colours. I choose the mug as carefully as I choose which tea would be best for her at the time.

As I serve her the tea, in rubber gloves, she takes a sip then tries to guess which tea I used. She shrieks in delight when she gets it right but then always wants to know why I have chosen that particular tea. If it is late at night, obviously I brew a cup that will induce sleep. I am careful how I explain it, though. "Princess, this tea is to make you sleep well and have sweet dreams." She delights in my answers so I play along.

Wet compound

❧

THIS FRIDAY we are hitting the nightlife in Riyadh, not that there is much of it, especially for women. Lea has contacted one of her expat friends. She has been working in Riyadh for years, and suggests we visit a wet compound – one that has a restaurant that serves alcohol. Smartly dressed under our abayas, and with much excitement at our first night out, we bundle into the waiting taxi. The buildings are lit up in a myriad colours. As drab as the city can seem in the day, it is beautiful at night.

We have a problem; my iqama, without which I cannot visit another compound, has not yet been issued. My passport, which would also be accepted, is being withheld. I ask the cab driver to take us to an internet cafe. We pull up to one that is completely empty. As I walk in, Lea following closely, two men walk hastily towards us. "No! You go!" says the younger one, closest to us. The older man seems more tolerant, but says, "You are not allowed in here. It is a men's only establishment, please go."

We are forced to retreat. I am determined, though. If I don't get a copy of my passport, which I have in an old email to the princess, I am going nowhere tonight. We are ushered out, but I ask the younger man whether I could print one page off an email, as the place is empty. He seems insulted as he slams the door behind me.

Regardless of age or marital status, a woman is required to have a male guardian. He may be her father, husband, uncle, brother – or even her own son. A woman cannot travel, attend university, work, or marry without her guardian's permission. In some cases, a woman cannot receive major medical treatment without the permission of her guardian.

The quality of life of a Saudi woman depends entirely on the male members of her family. If a woman is lucky enough to come from an open family, she will enjoy a free education, be encouraged to work if she chooses, have a say in who she marries, travel the world, and come and go as she pleases. If she comes from a more conservative family, she may not be allowed to do any of those things.

Next, we inquire at the international hotel on the corner. Friendly staff at reception lead me into their back office after I explain my urgency. Within two minutes, I have a copy of my passport.

We eventually reach the compound gates. It looks like a war zone. Since the compound bombings a decade before, most compounds have a heavy military presence and this one is no different. Every part of the taxi gets searched.

After passing through an office, we are thoroughly screened and our iqamas and the copy of my passport are held back. With permission, and after our visit is documented in two different large books, we are free to go. We walk out the other side of the small office, through a dark car park towards the lights.

The place is small and cosy with candles creating a magical ambience. Trellises with fake greenery afford some privacy between the tables. An Italian balladeer belts out tragic love songs from the speakers mounted on the ceiling. Small groups talk animatedly amid bursts of laughter. The only table available is situated in the centre of the restaurant. Not one man there fails to notice Lea's blonde hair. As most of the expats are from Middle Eastern countries, blonde hair is unusual and is leered at openly.

The taste of a gin and tonic is heaven on my tongue but heavy on the wallet. At SR40, it works out to R85 a drink. This doesn't deter us though. The Italian music creates a feeling of nostalgia that increases exponentially with each gin. Suddenly I feel invincible. I will make it in this crazy place!

As we are about to leave, a portly chef scuttles over to our table and suggests to Lea that we try the home made wine. At SR30 for half a glass, it does not come cheap but we all think, what the hell, in for a penny, in for a pound.

We arrive back at the compound, lighter in mood and in pocket and feeling much more positive than after the Starbucks experience of the previous week. Now I feel ready for the week ahead.

I knew it was coming

❦

THE FOLLOWING day I arrive at work to much activity. Over months the Filipino staff gather groceries, bought for them when Lilly goes out shopping for the princess. When their boxes are full, they ship them home to their families in the Philippines.

Each box is searched thoroughly by someone designated by the princess before it is sealed. The wizened old lady who accompanied me for my iqama medical sits on a chair leaning on a cane. She watches the girls like a hawk as every item is taken out of the boxes then repacked. There is hardly any talking. It is like a military operation. I escape into the kitchen to set up my laptop to continue the inventory.

I need to clarify something with the princess and as we are not allowed to phone her, I go up to her room. The door is closed and I knock softly in case she is sleeping. I hear her say "Mien" which I take for "Come in" and I open her bedroom door. She is dressed in tracksuit pants and a sleeveless vest. She looks furious and shouts "Get out!" For a moment

I am confused and before I can move towards the open door, she shouts again, "Get out!" Her arm is stretched out with her finger pointing towards the door.

I don't wait for her to repeat herself a third time. The bedroom door slams as I make my way downstairs. Not sure what just happened, I call Lilly aside. She explains that although, in Arabic "Meen" sounds very much like "Come in" it actually means "Who is there?"

I'd witnessed the way she treats her other staff, so I knew it was just a matter of time before she started on me. Although I was expecting it, I thought it would be over something a lot more serious than seeing her in a sleeveless T-shirt and sweat pants.

An hour later she calls me up. "Mrs C, you cannot come into my bedroom when I am naked!" she shouts. Naked? Only her arms were exposed. Think Black Hand. I apologise and briefly explain my mistake. It seems I have a lot to learn. She dismisses me with a wave of her hand. The encounter leaves me feeling slightly disgruntled as the outburst is completely out of proportion to the supposed offence.

Tonight the princess is expecting the manicurist, who waits downstairs. She asks me where South Africa is, which leads to an interesting conversation. I assure her there are no lions roaming in the streets. The princess calls me up first.

I knock softly and enter. The scowl has not left her face. "Mrs C, you are too friendly with the manicurist. She is here to do a job!" She says it so loudly I am sure the manicurist can hear her. I know better by now to say anything, so I retreat with "Yes, Your Highness."

The following day I start the library inventory. I have been looking forward to this. Although it's a back-breaking task as most of the work is done on a ladder, the variety of books keeps me going. The library is in the salon adjoining the princess's bedroom so I work quietly. I marvel at how clean all the books are and make a mental note to tell Sunny.

I categorise the books in more ways than one. I number the shelves, note the books as they appear and then document them by genre. It takes a long time as I cannot help reading bits or peeking into the many interesting books. Many self-help books fill the tightly packed shelves.

The wardrobe inventory will be a huge challenge. If you take all the clothing in stock at the average store and multiply that by at least five, it might come close to what the princess has. Her clothes are spread over four floors.

Part of the basement is taken up by a room the size of a basketball court, which is for clothing. It is locked at all times. The floor to ceiling cupboards, as well as another set in the centre of the room, are packed to the brim. The clothes hang so tightly together that it is almost impossible to remove an item without disturbing the whole cupboard.

On the first floor, another large room holds 20 two-metre-long rails lined up close together, covered by pristine white sheets that are changed weekly. There must be a couple of thousand garments.

The idea is to take a photo of each garment, front and back, and categorise it. I go upstairs to ask the princess if I may start the inventory – I need permission to enter these rooms. She is on a call but ends it as I knock. "Your Highness, I have finished the library. I'd like to start with the clothing inventory." She frowns terribly and chases me out. "I will tell you when to start!"

Farm visit

❧

MONA SPEAKS of going to the farm with much excitement. Although my family own a farm, the Amir and his entourage make more use of it than the women – they go to a farm belonging to the Amira's best friend, Princess Stephanie.

It is late Thursday afternoon. I phone switchboard, the mystery voice I deal with daily but never meet. He assures me that Sultan is ready and waiting outside.

The princess is having the finishing touches done to her braids so I go outside to check the car. The water bottles wrapped in serviettes are at the ready in the back pockets of the front seats. After spraying perfume onto her abaya at the last minute, we make our way downstairs. The walk to the car is strenuous as I am carrying the princess's many bags. I try hard to disguise my ragged breath as I settle next to her in the back seat.

It is dark outside as we leave the palace grounds. Eli swiftly closes the huge gates behind us. The princess is in a good mood.

Half an hour later, we pull up to tall gates. The staff jump into action – they are expecting us. The farm is not quite what I had expected. Extensive gardens, only half-planted, are surrounded by a high wall. A magnificent double-storey mansion is set towards the back of the grounds. Lights blaze from each room.

To the left, seven three-bedroom chalets house overnight guests. Sultan drives up to the five steps leading to the elevated patio of the main building. About 40 women are seated on large comfortable couches arranged in a square. The focal point is a large Persian carpet that covers the tiling. The princess joins her family on the patio while I am directed to one of the chalets that the princess will be using for the evening. I hang her abaya in the wardrobe and turn down her bed. After switching on a couple of side lamps, I make my way over to Mona.

It is a beautiful balmy evening and everyone seems relaxed. Soft Arabian music is playing in the background. I take the seat next to Mona and ask her about our roles on the farm. We just have to be visible, she explains; a butler is a status symbol within the Royal House of Saud. Well, visible we are. So we sit.

Dinner is served at 10. The hierarchy among staff is clearly evident. We are called to the buffet table after the royal family have dished up for themselves. As we make our way down the long line of tables, I marvel at the variety of dishes. The prawns are the size of baby crayfish. Only after we are seated do the nannies and teachers dish up, then last, the Filipino maids.

After dessert, the royals move inside to the largest lounge I have ever seen. Four chandeliers the size of king-sized beds adorn the vast ceiling. As Mona has been here before, I follow behind her, trying not to make eye contact with any of the women on the many couches. We are seated on the side of the lounge at a distance from the nearest royal but in full sight. This is ladies' night; for once the stiff formality is abandoned.

Mona and I can't really talk but we whisper to one another as I have many questions. Without making it obvious, I keep an eye on my princess because a subtle nod is all the warning I will have if she needs something. She is relaxed and it is a pleasure watching her interact with her many cousins.

After three hours of sitting, fighting to stay awake, tea, Arabian coffee and cake is served. This is one of the highlights of any dinner with the royals. Saudi cakes are out of this world, and there are at least 50 on the long table. This is not just for the 40 royals present, but for the staff as well – perhaps 60 of us.

I go for my favourite first, a fluffy concoction with lemon-flavoured candy floss between the layers. It is heavenly. The bitter taste of the Arabic coffee complements the sweetness of the cake.

It is now four in the morning and I catch my princess's eye as she beckons me. "You look exhausted. You can go if you like," she says with a smile. My eyes are still bloodshot and this often gives the impression that I am tired when I am not. Tonight I am. I thank her, wish her a pleasant evening and walk backwards for about 10 steps before turning. Mona is not at all impressed with what she sees as preferential treatment but then again she is employed by the Amira, not my princess.

As I go outside to the patio to collect my handbag and put on my abaya, I see another driver from our palace waiting at the edge of the expansive lawn. He speaks no English so the two previous times he collected us at the compound, we nodded in greeting. He is in the market van. At least it is bound to smell better at night when it is cooler; the heat only exacerbates the stench of fish.

Walking towards the steps, looking down and leaning slightly forward to get to the bottom buttons of my abaya, I stand on the front hem and feel myself falling forward. Instinctively I know I have the choice of throwing myself to the left into the newly turned flower bed with neat rows of little seedlings or to hit the concrete tiling, straight ahead, five steps down. I twist sideways, abaya billowing behind me, and land on all fours, sinking deeply into the fresh earth.

I hear an explosion coming from the waiting van. The driver thinks my undignified fall is hilarious. Still on all-fours I turn to see how many of the royals noticed. Fortunately I am out of their line of vision, the five steps towering above me, sheltering me. I collect the bits and pieces from my handbag that are scattered across the little seedlings. God forbid I miss a tampon (think pool noodle!). I stand up to dust myself off. Loud guffaws are still coming from the van.

The drive home is punctuated by the driver's sporadic bursts of laughter. I am glad it is dark in the car.

Desert Christmas

❧

FRIDAY ARRIVES; I am beyond excited. Besides being my birthday, it is also the day we join the Hash Club for Christmas carols in the desert. The email stated that no Arabs are allowed. Strange thing to just throw out there.

This is my first desert trip. I arrange to meet Mark at the gate at midday. We drive through the quiet city. Friday is the best day to explore Riyadh as it is the only time the traffic is not frenetic. We head into a part of the city I haven't seen and I say a silent prayer of thanks that I was placed in the suburb that I was. Mark talks non-stop, relishing his role as guide.

First we pick up Gail, an American colleague of Mark, then Linda, another colleague and also a fellow Brit. On the trip into the desert, they complain about their jobs, the difficult students and the long hours. Long hours, really? They work from nine to four and get two days off a week, allowing them to plan hiking and camping trips into the desert on weekends. Eventually one of them asks what I am doing in Riyadh. They are surprised at my working hours and conclude that they are rather well off.

We reach the outskirts of the desert where there is an SR20 entrance fee that includes a choice of two meals. Expats from all over the world have gathered here today. There are three hikes before lunch, a short 10-minute one, a medium hike of 50 minutes and a rather long and strenuous one of an hour and a half. Mark, a long distance runner, goes for the long one. I play it safe and join the medium group.

We make our way over a rocky hill. The desert is beautiful. After the congestion of the city, the wide open expanse feels wonderful. Midway, we are given oranges and a soft drink. I hear Afrikaans being spoken behind me. I turn to greet the blonde woman in her forties. With much excitement, we swop stories. She is an English teacher. She also complains about the unwilling students but it feels good to interact with someone from home. It is short-lived as we start making our way back.

Groups of picnickers are already scattered round, blankets strewn over the desert sand. Huge bonfires are stacked, ready for the evening. Lines form at the two food tents, for good old boerie rolls with relish or a lamb Schwarma. The aroma of spices coming from the Schwarma tent is far more exotic so I join that queue. The lamb is delicious.

— 110 —

I guess there must be over a thousand people. I saw this occasion as the ideal way to meet other expats, but everyone is in groups, sticking to those they know. I join Gail and Linda and spread my blanket next to them. They seem friendly enough but are so deep in conversation, I don't interrupt. They are discussing their love lives. Being privy to their personal conversation, I feel like an intruder. It is starting to get dark and I watch as the organisers set up the Christmas tree lights and light the hundreds of candles in bags of different colours. The effect is beautiful. The hill in front of us is aglow.

I am still in the same spot, but I've given up on trying to make conversation with the two girls I came with. They are not that interested in what is happening beyond their immediate circle. Mark is involved with the lighting so is scarce for the better part of the day.

Singing along to the Christmas carols brings a lump to my throat; it makes me miss home. So much for celebrating my birthday today. No one even knows it is my birthday. I must confess to a moment of self-pity but at the same time feel a little foolish as I'm not usually the type to indulge it. Still, the feeling refuses to leave me.

Linda and Gail excuse themselves and return 10 minutes later with three Styrofoam cups of glühwein. It is piping hot and has something rather strong in it but warms me up nicely in the now chilly desert. I sip it sparingly.

The bonfires are lit. Rock music has replaced the carols. Still I sit in our spot, conversation scarce and my derrière, numb. I go back to the glühwein table. The queue is long but moves quickly. I smile broadly as I tell the woman serving, "Please may I have another one. It's my birthday today." As I say it I realise how pathetic it sounds. For who knows what reason, I felt the need to tell at least one person. The woman replies, "You're welcome to have another; you don't have to have an excuse." Ouch. That was not my intention. Perhaps I just needed to hear one person say "Happy birthday", as silly as that seems.

An icy wind starts up, blowing the embers of the many fires into the crowds. There is a steady stream of headlights as people leave . We wait until last while Mark dismantles the lights. It seems to take forever. I am feeling cold, tired and down. I am among hundreds of people but it just emphasises my loneliness.

I get a text message alert on my mobile and am surprised and delighted with the message from the princess.

"Happy Happy Birthday Mrs C! Hope this year & all ur coming years be filled with peace, love, success & prosperity!

Hope ur enjoying ur special day. Eat looooots of cake for both of us hehehe. Thx 4 being here with me & 4 taking care of me, really appreciate it. Luv u lots & GOD BLESS xoxo."

Will the princess ever know that her message made my day?

I don't say much on the trip home apart from thanking Mark for inviting me.

As I get back to the compound at 11, I hear laughter and music at the pool. It sounds so inviting but I don't go. Mona is watching TV in the lounge so I escape to my bedroom to watch a movie on my laptop with earphones on as the TV is blaring.

Although I did not meet any new people, I am grateful that I could spend the day outside the compound. Despite my bout of self-pity, it was an amazing experience.

Week three

❧

TODAY I am cooking for the princess. She asked but does not have an inkling what's on the menu. I tell her she has to trust me as it is a surprise. By now I have learnt what she likes and what she doesn't. I make a rich savoury mince inside a red bell pepper, topped with grilled cheese. I sweeten the butternut slightly and add a pinch of cinnamon. I pipe the puréed butternut onto her plate in a swirl. I add a small side salad with my homemade citrus dressing.

One of the girls sets a tray with the princess's special crockery and cutlery, which is kept in her kitchen upstairs. I am tempted to put a flower on the tray but the princess is so deathly scared of any insects that all the plants in her villa are fake. "Real plants bring insects," she explains. I put on the rubber gloves and take her tray upstairs.

Mona is with the princess. As I enter the bedroom, I notice that she scrutinises the plate of food. No doubt she could do it better. The look on her face reveals that she doesn't like the fact that the princess seems excited at the prospect of my cooking.

Lilly places a towel on her bed to protect the linen and the tray is placed in front of her. She looks happy and a little intrigued. I wish her a pleasant meal and leave the room.

Half an hour later I am called up. Mona is still with the princess and is scowling as the princess raves about the dinner.

At half past 11, I arrive at our compound. I am tired, and relieved to be home after a long day. As I walk through the gate, I bump into Serge and a friend on their way to the pool bar. His exuberant pleasure at our accidental meeting is so obvious that I allow myself to be persuaded to join them for coffee. I ask for 10 minutes to unload the abaya and change into something casual. (With a spritz of perfume.)

He is the first to see me nearing from a distance. His smile says it all. The chemistry takes up where we left off with a vengeance and with no regard for whether both parties want to play. His gentleness and ability to make me laugh when I least expect to endear him to me. I had not intended to feel this way toward anyone in this strange country.

Once again, Serge stands up when I get up to leave. He leans in and kisses me on both cheeks.

Mona arrives home an hour after me. She is in a foul mood as once again as she was not paid on time. Our contracts state that we are paid on the first of every month. It has never been a problem so far but tonight, Mona is looking for any excuse to rant about the royals. So she will get paid tomorrow, on the 3rd. It is not as if she is starving.

"Arabella (as she calls the princess when we are alone) bloody well exhausts me!" she says as she puts her bags down." Why do I have to sit with her and listen to all her crap?!" I say nothing but can't help thinking, "Oh Mona, cut the act."

I get ready for bed but Mona has one more thing to add: "Oh by the way, I have to mention to you that there is a layer of dust on the white chandeliers in the entrance hall so you'd better see to it tomorrow before the princess sees it."

I am torn between thanking her kindly and telling her to fuck off. It seems I am catching on to the universal language that also seems common in Saudi. I know for a fact that the chandeliers are cleaned every day. I saw Sunny on the ladder earlier on in the day. Mona's insecurities really bring the worst out in her.

Mona

❧

I CAN sense that Mona is not too enamoured about my budding friendship with Serge. Up to now, though, she hasn't dared say anything.

At home, there is no space for my groceries in the freezer as it is packed with little tidbits of leftover food that Mona has hoarded over time. Some bits are as small as matchboxes, all neatly wrapped in foil. Only she would know what these are. Four boxes of old chips, bought with KFC chicken months ago, take pride of place in the freezer door.

I close a blind, she opens it. God help me if I put a dish back in the wrong place. I understand that Mona is a perfectionist but she is of the type that spend their lives trying to drag people up to their standards. What makes their beliefs standards? I am seething. We are heading for a showdown that has been building up for a while.

Another bone of contention is that Mona invites a lot of people over every Friday so the day can never be spent relaxing in a peaceful environment. Mona also feels compelled to feed the guests breakfast and lunch. The constant clanging of dishes and loud voices rules out an occasional afternoon nap, such a luxury with the long hours we work. Watching TV is also out as Mona feels that it is noisy, and a conversation killer. An adder is slowly making its way up my spine.

Curiouser and curiouser

❧

I ARRIVE at work to be informed by Lilly that the princess is getting ready for another appointment. While I wait to be called up, I take the ladder out. Balancing on the top rung, I check all the chandeliers in the entrance hall and the two in the lounge. They are spotless, as I knew they would be.

Is it a coincidence that Mona comes in a little later with a tray of special eats she had made for the princess after I left home? I think not.

Lilly steams the princess's abaya and after spraying it with perfume, it is hung outside the princess's door. I suddenly realise with a sinking feeling that I did not bring an extra pair of sandals as I always do. I am wearing Crocs, which I remove when I enter the villa. Many a day I put my shoes or sandals back on only when it is time to go home.

Lilly keeps looking at my feet. She offers me a pair of her shoes but they are far too small. I will just have to try and hide the offending shoes with my abaya. The princess steps out of her room and I stand ready, holding her abaya, I help her get into it. She is not in a good mood. We complete the dressing in silence. I make sure I walk a good couple of steps behind her.

Sultan is ready as usual and opens the car door for the princess. The smell of perfume in the car is so overwhelming that I can hardly breathe. We are about five minutes into our journey when the princess spots the Crocs. "What are those?!" she shouts, pointing at my feet. I try to explain. She explodes into a rage. "What are you thinking going out with me in such shoes?!" She is looking at me with unbridled disgust. All I can do is apologise. I am now the one who is called an imbecile by the princess. She clicks her tongue a couple of times and shakes her head from side to side to emphasise her unhappiness.

Clucking her tongue and shaking her head while looking at you as if you have just crept out of a bin when she is displeased is the one thing the princess does that drives me nuts. Mona says she has learnt this habit from the Amir. It is so insulting that you can't help but bristle at it.

Just after my apology, Sultan brakes a bit sharply, jerking both of us forward in the back seat. The princess fires off a barrage of insults in Arabic and his soft answer is lost to me. She clucks her tongue again and mutters "idiot" under her breath. It must be an interesting journey, being accompanied by an imbecile and an idiot.

The princess steps out of the car, swathed in black, the huge sunglasses firmly in place. I don't quite understand what the fuss is about as she is so unrecognisable and she herself is wearing sneakers.

She is walking fast and I battle to keep up with her but I make sure the door opening goes off smoothly. The princess is so annoyed as we get to the lift that she pushes the button herself. With her elbow. The lift takes too long so we walk up the stairs to the first floor reception. Who takes a lift for one floor anyway, I think. Thank goodness the doctor is available immediately so the princess is escorted into his rooms. I settle in for a long wait. The kindle is fully charged.

There is no conversation on the way home. I fix my gaze out of my window. As we get to the palace, she abruptly opens the car door herself and strides towards her villa. Now, I keep to about 10 paces behind her. I am not there to open the front door for her. I am an imbecile.

Lilly calls me into her room where my bright new uniforms are hanging on cheap coat hangers. My God, they are ghastly!

I arrive home with the stack of uniforms draped over my arm. Mona doesn't hide her delight as she laughs at the multi-coloured, shapeless uniforms. This just confirms her nastiness but I choose to ignore it. "You look like an inmate," she laughs as I disappear into the shower, offering no response.

It is still relatively early so we go out to the pool for a coffee. I tell her what happened. "Never forget, it is us against them!" she says with passion. Something she repeats often. I marvel at the different roles Mona plays. At home she rants against the behaviour of the royals but at work she acts like a saint. Her excessive sweetness with my princess galls me, as she speaks scathingly about her at home,

Living with Mona has become almost unbearable. She still sees the flat as hers. I suggested we get a pot plant or two and she replied with, "Well, we will see." I get a pot plant for my room and leave it at that.

One day Mona gets home two hours after me, livid. "Princess Arabella stole my identity!" I get out of bed and put the kettle on while Mona changes out of her work clothes. She explains. An American doctor offers a special, individualised diet on the basis of responses to an intensive online questionnaire. After the princess had listed all her ailments, she was turned down for the programme. She re-entered, using Mona's home address and identity.

Mona tells me the princess has been pestering two German girls, scrutinising their Facebook profiles daily. She wants them to work for her and cannot accept that they turned her down. What the princess doesn't know is that Mona knows both girls personally. Every time the princess tells Mona to phone them to try to change their minds, Mona does the opposite, warning them, telling them not to accept the princess's offer.

One day there is a threatening message on the princess's timeline written by one of the girls. The princess freaks out. She asks me if they will be able to see how many times someone has looked at their Facebook profile. "I am not certain but will try and find out," I assure her. She is actually scared. I phone my nephew, an IT specialist in Cape Town and he assures me you cannot, but you can be traced by the IP address, right to the chair you are sitting on. This stops the princess in her tracks; she gives up on them.

I speak to a good looking Syrian in his early thirties at the pool that evening. The others call him "the Playboy" as he tries to seduce any new girl at the compound. More often than not, his pursuits are successful. He mentions that there is a one-bedroom flat going vacant. I discreetly ask him for the details. He tells me he has the contact number for the owner at his flat. We make an arrangement to meet at his apartment the following day.

He welcomes me to his flat as if he is starved for conversation. He offers me coffee and cookies, and takes out a bowl of crisps and peanuts. The coffee table in the lounge resembles a picnic although I am only there to pick up the number. He suddenly gets up from the chair he is sitting on and joins me on the two-seater couch.

We make small talk till he suddenly leans over and hugs me. It seems innocent enough so I briefly hug him back. He doesn't let go. I pull myself away and stand up to leave. At the door, he pulls me into a hug that is far too close for comfort – he is pushing his groin into me. I pull away quite forcefully and tell him Mona is waiting for me. On the way back to my flat with a crumpled piece of paper clutched in my sweaty hand, I marvel at how brazen this man is.

I join Mona at the kitchen table and jump right in. "There is a one-bedroom flat going vacant and I am going to speak to the princess about it." Mona's eyes are wide as she stutters, "Um, um, the princess will never allow it. She complains about the cost of this apartment every month. It's not a good idea!" By now I can read Mona so much better; she is afraid that the princess will find out what a bully she has been. I can clearly see it on her face. All I offer as I get up to get ready for work is, "Well, we will see."

The last thing I hear before I close the bathroom door is Mona repeating, "It is not a good idea!" She is worried about the princess finding out why I want to move into my own place. One thing I know, the princess will not be tolerant of Mona's territorial behaviour.

Desert dinner

PRINCESS ARABELLA calls me up to her room. She is in a happy mood and childlike in her excitement as she tells me to prepare as we are heading into the desert tomorrow evening. No travelling arrangement is discussed with any of the staff until the day before an event. This is a safety precaution, adhered to strictly by the entire extended royal family. It makes for an extremely stressful time for the staff lower on the hierarchy as they have to get everything together in a couple of hours.

My princess's preparations start early in the morning. Outfit after outfit is brought up from the basement as she decides what to wear for the night. By the time she has made a selection, every available surface in her vast bedroom is covered with piles of discarded clothes.

"Dress warmly," she says, smiling from ear to ear. She is sitting crossed-legged on her bed, her knees bouncing up and down as she excitedly tells me what to expect. She is so utterly endearing when she is in this mood. How I wish I could reach her and show her that there is more to life than this gilded cage. Her nasty moods are embedded in past hurts that she clings to as tightly as she does to Allah.

The drivers are on standby and start at six in the morning, carting truckloads of goods to kit out the royal tents in the desert. Persian carpets, pillows, music systems, snacks, exquisite chocolates and enough soft drinks for a month. We accompany our individual princesses in their cars and the royal convoy sets out for the desert at around two in the afternoon.

The princess is suddenly in a bad mood and sits staring sullenly out of the window. Apart from shouting at the driver a couple of times, she does not utter a word which dampens my excitement but that is not my main concern. When she is like this, huge issues can arise at any time, whether imagined or real.

Every time we hit a bump, she shakes her head and clucks her tongue. After an hour and a half of travelling, 30 minutes of it extremely bumpy as there is no specific road to follow, we arrive at the camping site. I help the princess out and take her abaya and handbag for safekeeping. We have not spoken one word during the trip. I have a knot in my stomach. It is late afternoon and I have no way of knowing how long we will be in the desert.

I have asked Serge to feed the cats tonight although I know that, after living in Saudi for almost 20 years, he probably feels the same way about them as the locals. At least he has the good sense not to admit it to me.

Several large tents are dotted around a huge sand dune. The vast desert stretches out from it as far as you can see. One of the tents, with plump pillows strewn around, is the men's lounge for the drivers and other male staff. Huge bonfires are stacked and ready for the cold desert night.

The main tent for the royals is a beautiful dark red with a gold leaf pattern spreading across the ceiling. Fairy lights are wrapped around the wooden poles that bring electricity to the tent. The beautiful Persian carpets overlap to allow no sand in and large grass bowls of assorted chocolates and snacks are placed within reach of the seating. Once everyone is seated on the pillows on the carpets, a vibey Arabian rock song starts playing. Mona and I look at one another and smile. Prince Abdullah is at the controls.

The women make themselves comfortable in the main tent and I watch as all the men line up outside, facing Mecca for the afternoon prayer. It is a hauntingly beautiful sight as they go down on their knees and touch their foreheads to the sand.

Once the royals are settled, Mona and I explore the individual tents erected for preparations. A beautiful goat is enclosed in a pen. It does not take much to guess where Billy the kid is heading. I stroke its fluffy head. The light brown eyes looking up at me are knowing. Two magnificent horses are tied up to a nearby pole in waiting for any of the royals who would like to take a ride. Four quad bikes are parked close by for the amusement of the royals' children.

I am surprised to see two toilets, not unlike the hired ones seen on construction sites standing, about a hundred metres from the nearest tent. There is no toilet for the men, and one is for the royal family only. A hose hangs next to them. Every toilet in Saudi either has a bidet or a hose. The hose in our flat is cold water only.

Two chefs from a local restaurant in Riyadh come out at about 10 to start preparing the food on huge open fires outside the dining tent. They are Syrian, both very attractive young men and outrageous flirts. Mona and I spend some time bantering with them.

We are positioned near the entrance in case we are needed as the royal family are seated inside, having their dinner. The food – spicy beef kebabs, steak strips and lamb chops – comes in off the fire at regular intervals. There are platters of the traditional Middle Eastern hummous, baba ganoush and tabouleh salad that accompany almost every meal and there in the middle of them lies Billy, in pieces, on a disc of rice about a metre in diameter.

We are called in for dinner next. Once again, the hierarchy is strictly followed. After the royal family, the PAs dine next and once we are finished, we call the teachers and nannies. After them are the Filipino servants and only then do the men take over the dining tent. No woman is allowed inside while they eat.

It is now two o'clock in the morning and it is freezing. After supervising the clean up in the dining tent, Mona and I join the royals in the main tent. Our job is to sit and wait. We chat and eat chocolate, the only way we can stay awake. Sitting for hours on end doing nothing is difficult, especially for an A-type personality, but fighting to stay awake is even more difficult.

Prince Abdullah walks over to where Mona and I are sitting. He holds his hand out to me and I blindly take what he is offering. Next he passes some to Mona. It is Bedouin bread that the prince has baked himself on the open fire. It is delicious. "I have been fed from the hands of a prince; I can happily die now" I tell Mona as we both dissolve in a fit of giggles.

The princesses are dancing in a slow, sensuous rhythm, all moving in one direction then turning simultaneously, their arms forming patterns in the air. It is a pleasure to watch. Each woman seems to be lost in her own world while weaving back and forth.

For a moment I focus on the Amira, my princess's mother. She is the most beautiful and graceful woman I have met in a long time. At all times this princess is the epitome of a lady. She looks years younger than her 40-something age and her dress sense borders on bohemian. I am fascinated by her. She has a gliding walk and I love the fact that wherever she sits she puts her legs up and tucks her feet under her. She always has a smile and laughs readily.

The haunting Arabic melodies reach far into the desert night. I get a text message from Serge, "Princess Sahara, when will you be home? I am missing you ..." My smile lingers long after the message is read.

Again Prince Abdullah makes his way over to where we are sitting and again his outstretched arm offers a secret delight. I take it from his hand and wait for Mona to receive hers before I look at what we've been given. In my hand lies a pinkish piece of liver from Billy the goat. I look at Mona with big eyes while the prince towers over us, waiting for us to eat it.

Mona takes a bite as if it is the tastiest morsel she has ever eaten. Did I mention that she is smitten with the prince? The cold piece of liver lies heavily in my hand. I am next so I close my eyes and take a small bite. It is not pleasant; it is actually one of the grossest things I have ever tasted. I smile up at the prince as my fantasy dies a horrible death. No amount of 7Up can wash the taste from my mouth.

At four in the morning, platters of cakes are brought in with strong Arabic coffee. This is a ritual that takes place daily. A staggering variety of cakes, one outdoing the other is spread out in a lavish display, as well as trays of desserts. One of the Filipino girls from the main palace, by order of the princess, dishes up for us and presents us with two plates stacked with at least six slices of cake each. I had forgotten that this is how the royals do it – dish up large servings, have a mouthful or two from each slice, and discard the rest.

After the cake, there's another stretch of about an hour of just sitting. "I am so cold that if the Mutawa drove past, I'd willingly give myself up for 50 lashes because at least that would warm me up!" I say, through chattering teeth. We are so tired that my comment sets off a fit of giggles. And after that we are in hysterics at the smallest thing. Discreetly of course.

At six, I get the nod from a Filipino staff member from the main palace. I fetch the princess's belongings from the "women's tent". At half past six, the drivers line up the cars and we start the trek back to the palace.

Much of the staff stays behind to pack up. This is a job that will take the better part of the day and Mona and I are relieved that we are spared this as it is Friday morning – and our day off.

The princess is tired but seems in a better mood than when we arrived and for that I am grateful. She throws a "Nighty night, Mrs C" over her shoulder as I close the front door behind her. Sultan is ready to take me home. I am frozen to the bone and tired. As we pass the gates, Eli smiles at me as he makes eye contact through my open window. As we leave the palace grounds, I wind the window up.

I'd learned, the hard way, that women are not allowed to drive in a car with a window open. When I turned the window down on one of the main routes home, Sultan almost flipped the car in his haste to close it with one arm bent backward at an unnatural angle, pumping the handle, trying to drive with the other.

We get home at 10 o'clock. Serge has invited me to stop by for coffee on my way in. I decline, but agree to meet up later in the day. Even though today is Friday, we sleep away the better part of the day.

Feeling refreshed and wide awake after the deep sleep, I hit the shower. As I lather the shampoo, I eagerly anticipate the prospect of an afternoon with Serge.

At five, Mona and I join Serge at the pool. It is a gentle afternoon with much laughter. Mona's guests have once again joined us. The smell of shisha pipes and the Arabian music from the huge TV mounted to the boundary wall makes for a heady combination. I almost make a point of keeping my distance from Serge. Yet his eyes never leave me. At eight, after too many coffees, I excuse myself, wish everyone a pleasant night, and go to feed the cats.

As I empty the last of the pellets out of the bowl, a woman speaks right behind me in a loud voice, startling me. "Why you feed these cats?" she asks, in an annoyed tone. "No good feeding these cats," she says. "No, no, no good," she says again, emphatically. I turn around to see a local Saudi woman in her early twenties, quite plump from all the food she has to eat.

Right at that moment, Mr Grey hurtles up to me but as he passes the woman, she kicks out at him. Although she narrowly misses him, I see red. I unleash all the hurt and fury I have felt at the mistreatment of cats in Saudi Arabia on her.

She did not see this coming and takes a few steps back at my outpour. "What the hell has it got to do with you if I choose to feed them?! Look at them, for God's sake, they are starving!" I glare at her but she says nothing. "You disgust me. You should be ashamed of yourself," I end off, before turning back to the compound with Mr Grey at my feet, walking me to the compound door, as he always does.

On a roll

❧

SO WE start a new week. I have a lot of enthusiastic plans to ensure that it goes off as smoothly as possible. Once at work, I put in an order to the main palace for the ingredients I'll need for the princess's dinner tonight.

I am served dinner at the villa every night. At four in the afternoon, Lilly collects my tray from the chalet kitchen. The first couple of times I can only stare at all the food in shock. Three trays, one with four different pastas, another heaped with savoury pastries and at least three different salads, and the last tray so packed with meat that it could easily feed 10 people. Grilled chicken, grilled fish, a couple of pieces of steak and lamb kebabs fill the tray.

After a couple of weeks of this, I ask Lilly to be more selective and bring me less food. Yet, with all the good food I still lose five kilograms during my first month in Saudi. The princess laughingly envies my weight loss. I don't doubt the adjustment to the heat had something to do with it.

I am making chicken pie with a few accompanying dishes.

As I position the puff pastry over the chicken, I keep some of the dough aside. In an attempt to pull off the wow factor, as we were taught at the academy, I cut out the letters PA, for Princess Arabella from the leftover dough and place the letters on top of the pie crust. I place a dish of baby marrows in a cream sauce in the oven alongside the pie. So far so good. The girls are bustling around the busy kitchen in order to see the outcome.

The princess lets Lilly know that she is ready to be served. The tray is carried upstairs and I must admit, the food looks scrumptious.

The princess watches in silence as Lilly puts down the towel in preparation as I stand waiting to place the tray onto her bed. As she gets a better view of the tray, she claps her hands together. "Mrs C, that looks wonderful!" she responds gleefully.

I wish her bon appétit and feeling happy, I leave her to enjoy her dinner.

On the trip home, I sit in silence, feeling contented with how the day went but also relieved that it had ended on such a happy note.

Apart from the princess periodically shouting at the staff, the week progresses without any incident so serious that it is deemed to deserve punishment. For that I am grateful.

I dedicate one day to laundry duties. The pieces of the princess's clothing that need to go to Madam Lorraine, the dressmaker, for alterations are put to one side. Lilly calls switchboard and asks Sultan to collect the clothes. We unpack the many shelves that have become slightly disarrayed and repack the contents in groups. Lilly watches with big eyes as I empty the overflowing vacuum cleaner. I show her step by step how to clean the vacuum bag. Next I show her how to clean the filters in the washing machine and tumble dryer. I am happy that Lilly looks impressed.

On Thursday the princess calls me up to her room. She is in a wonderful mood and I bask in it while it lasts. She has stacked some of her designer handbags in a corner and tells me that I am welcome to them. "They are real designer bags," she tells me as if that should mean something to me. I have never been a label orientated person but two of the bags are beautiful and I thank her profusely, as she would expect.

Some of the bags have seen better days but it would not be correct to turn them down. A variety of elaborate scarves, also for me, lie in a pile on her bed.

As an afterthought, the princess adds, "Don't tell Mrs M that I gave them to you." I feel a surge of irritation and before I can stop myself, I blurt out, "What my employer decides to give me has nothing to do with Mrs M!" I am surprised when the princess laughs out loud and replies, "Mrs C, I like you!"

Anyway, it is not possible to hide such a large stash of goods from Mona as we leave the palace together at the end of the evening. I do however offer Mona the bags I know I won't use and I throw in some scarves just to keep the peace.

All in all it is a good week and I happily look forward to my day off.

Friday

FRIDAY MORNING I bound out of bed while the whole world is still asleep. As they work until midnight, socialising until all hours of the morning is commonplace. Most of the Arab nation sleeps away the better part of the next day and the expats follow suit so at eight, I feel as if I have the compound to myself.

These early mornings have become my favourite time of the day. I wake around seven and Mona sleeps until at least 11 most mornings. As I don't want to disturb her, I take my laptop and a cup of coffee and sit at the pool. It is deserted at that time of the morning and I love the solitude. Apart from the call to prayer that breaks the stillness of the morning, nothing moves. A previous king declared that every man, no matter how poor, should have access to a mosque for prayers so they are all within walking distance of one another. At the announcement of the call to prayer, you hear the singing from at least five mosques at once.

I am laughing at the emails of friends and loving the prospect of having the day off. Today I am downloading a couple of documentaries on South Africa for the princess. During one of our chats, I asked her if I could accompany her to South Africa for a visit. The princess laughed at my suggestion, saying her father would never allow it.

Two weeks ago Mona came across a recipe for pineapple beer on the Internet and we decided to test it. Our first and second batches of seven litres were greatly welcomed and applauded by our friends. It tastes like cider and is refreshing in the heat. Initially it created quite a mess as the stickiness was hard to remove from the floors even after mopping several times over, but now the operation is smooth and effortless. All that is needed is yeast, pineapples, sugar, raisins and lukewarm water.

We have organised a barbeque this afternoon with our new friends from last week. I am in a terrific mood at the prospect of normality. The week before, Mona and I brewed up a triple quantity of pineapple beer. It was an extremely good batch and began bubbling just hours after completion. Six days later we decant it into one and a half litre plastic bottles. The recipe says decant after three days.

We emptied the fridge of groceries as the 20 litres of highly explosive pineapple beer takes pride of place. We are to learn that the longer pineapple beer stands, the stronger it gets. It develops a fizziness that is refreshing but also dangerous if left out of the fridge as the tops tend to blow off. A hilarious fact that saw a friend hit the floor when the first one popped. Out of the fridge, the plastic bottles swell up to such a degree that they fall over as the bottle bulges like a rugby ball.

When I opened one of these, the plastic top shot off, slamming into my hand. Within 10 minutes, I had a lump on the side of my hand the size of a golf ball. The princess, alarmed at seeing the huge bruise and swelling on my hand the following day, was quick to inquire what happened. With fingers crossed behind my back, I told her I had tripped over my abaya. This happens regularly so I don't feel too bad about the untruth.

The subtle seduction that seems to be ongoing is also not far from my mind. I am looking forward to seeing Serge again. Back at the flat, Mona has started breakfast and also seems to be in a good mood which enhances my happiness.

After a leisurely morning, we make our way outside. The greeting is warm and welcoming. Hugs all round. The guys provide the meat and a couple of bottles of wine. We proudly present our offering of salads, cheese platters and pineapple beer, which draws a lot of interest and admiration.

He is last in line to be greeted. We kiss on both cheeks, and he sneaks in a third as I pull away. He tells me that in Lebanon everyone kisses three times. The other Lebanese guys laugh at the obvious lie. My God, he smells good. He looks at me with a boyish grin as he pulls out the chair next to him. The platters are largely ignored. We are encouraged to have some of their wine as they sample the pineapple "juice".

It is a delightful afternoon with easy chatter getting rowdier as the juice levels drop. He is never far from my side.

Many discussions bounce around the table. I listen to the Lebanese guys discussing Saudi women. Every one of them has had a short-term sexual relationship with a Saudi woman. Local women who are virgins only participate in anal sex as they have to be virgins if they want to marry a Muslim man. The guys don't seem to mind. For the local woman who are divorced, this obviously doesn't apply.

Arab women are beautiful – there's no mistaking their allure. The only way these women are able to express their individuality is through their handbags, shoes and sunglasses. I often see women at Tamimi's wearing sequined stiletto sandals, their feet immaculately pedicured.

We have regrouped and again Serge pulls out the chair for me right next to him. His crystal rosary is a great ice-breaker.

He takes my hand into his to demonstrate how to hold the rosary so the beads glide easily. He smiles at my clumsiness – the result of him holding my hand. There is no denying the current that passes between us, unnoticed by the others. The expression on his face confirms that he has heard my sharp intake of breath and he looks at me searchingly.

It is late; I need to think. I excuse myself and say my good-byes. He invites me to tea at his flat tomorrow evening after work. Although he lives only two doors down, the invitation promises entry into a whole new world. I accept. We exchange numbers.

My logic fights this attraction. I see the pitfalls and com-plications, time constraints and illegalities. It's just tea, I think. I don't even have to take R10 for a taxi, as my father made me do years ago when I started dating in college.

I give Serge no more thought as Saturday morning hits with a vengeance. The copious amounts of vitamin C imbibed the day before is taking its toll. Even Mona is quiet for once. She makes us omelettes for lunch, I ask for mine blander than usual. Lethargic and reluctant, we get ready for work at four.

Lockdown

❧

THE DRIVE to the palace is a stressful one as we are collected in the van that transports fish and fresh vegetables from the market at the crack of dawn. The palace cars are unavailable because the Amir has gone to the farm for the evening. The amount of staff, luggage, food and luxuries that are taken with on such a trip, even just for one night, leaves the royal women disgruntled as there are no drivers left to pander to their demands.

The heat and the stench in the van turn my stomach but I manage to hold myself together.

As I enter the villa, I immediately sense the tension. The girls are scurrying around, absorbed in their own thoughts and not easily drawn into answering my probing questions. I am trying to find out what the problem is but no one is talking. I've learnt that when the staff are behaving like this, it means the princess has woken up in a bad mood, which severely affects how she treats them. I change out of my abaya and before I start my rounds, I go up to greet the princess. Her door is closed. This is never a good sign.

I start up in the laundry. As usual, Lilly accompanies me as we go through the day's laundry and dry cleaning list. Her dedication amazes me. She refuses to look at me. I can see that she has been crying. No matter how hard I try, I cannot get anything out of them. They seem scared to death.

At half past six, Lilly comes down to the kitchen and informs us that the princess wants us to gather in the pool house for a meeting. She will join us in 15 minutes'. I grab my notebook and pen, happy that there is some action to follow yet with an unease I can't explain. The girls wait inside the lavishly decorated pool room while I sit at the patio table outside. Fifteen minutes pass slowly, then I hear the unmistakable click of the front door. We are locked out. I call Lilly and when I tell her this, she looks terrified. Obviously they know something I don't. Has this happened to them before? She is evasive.

An hour and a half passes. I keep myself busy with the lists in my notebook in case the princess makes an appearance but I am sure this was never her intention. Suddenly piercing screams and what sounds like sobbing come from the princess's room. After two hours, we are called back inside. I have a call from switchboard advising me that the driver is at the main gate, waiting to take me home. I am still clueless.

I find it strange that my bag is not quite in the same place as I left it when I arrived. Before I leave the villa, I go upstairs to say goodnight to the princess but her door is closed. I can't get out of there fast enough. I head straight downstairs to pack up my laptop. There is a text message waiting for me, "I am waiting for you on the gate with cake." Oh my God, I had completely forgotten that I would be meeting up with Serge tonight. On the gate?

The traffic is not as congested as usual and sooner rather than later we arrive at the compound. I am tense as I try to make sense of what has happened tonight. I don't think meeting up with Serge now is good timing but at the same time, I can't cancel. It is, after all, just tea. Another text message has me laughing as I read, "Captain and crew awaiting your arrival . . ." Perhaps this won't be too bad, though the timing could have been better.

I freshen up and change into something comfortable. As I come around the corner, I am surprised to find Serge standing in the doorway of the passage leading to his flat, with a smile so sweet and an arm outstretched to take my hand. He leads me into his flat. I follow him into the lounge where he suddenly turns for the customary kisses on the cheek. His smell eradicates the last of my common sense.

Twelve cupcakes in assorted flavours line the coffee table. That's not unusual but Serge doesn't eat cake so it is all for me. My love for tiramisu is born. Much to my delight, the quiet man at the pool turns out to be quite a conversationalist and comedian. We laugh often, and I note his good manners with pleasure.

He tells me about his family life in Lebanon. I am mesmerised. He shares stories of the joys and ordeals of producing the yearly quota of arak on the family farm.

I go very still when he says that he is still married, though he and his wife have been separated for three years. The reason that neither of them has filed for divorce is that they are not only Catholics but Maronites.

Traditionally, Maronites are the most powerful. According to the Lebanese constitution, they hold the Lebanese presidency. Divorce is forbidden for Maronites.

Their house is rented out; his wife has moved back to the family farm where her parents live. When Serge goes home, he stays on his parents' farm. He has two children, a daughter of 19 and a son aged 17, in his last year of school. They are a family of architects and lawyers, his daughter just entering her first year of architecture at the University of Lebanon.

His son is a racing fan. Although he doesn't yet race, he

dreams of doing this, a nightmare for Serge. He throws his hands in the air, grinning broadly as he says his son his headstrong. Serge beams when he speaks about them.

After two cups of tea, we progress from the uncomfortable Victorian couch to the floor onto duvets and pillows Serge has piled around. At four in the morning, we are still absorbed in conversation but what I am likely to face in a couple of hours' time forces me to call it a night – or, more accurately a morning. How fast time flies when I am with him.

The following day...

ONE DAY at the palace is as good as the next is a nightmare. Not knowing what I'm about to face cements the knot in my stomach. A day may start well only for something to set the princess off. Her voice carries as far as the main palace as she screams at the staff. Bad moods can last for days on end. It is like walking a tight rope. Every day there is an underlying tension in the villa that is briefly relieved when the princess has a good day. My spastic colon is having a field day.

When I arrive at the palace, the staff are not in the basement. I go up to greet the princess to find the four girls sitting on the carpet next to the princess's bed. She has a terrible scowl on her face. She tells me, in front of them, that they all deserve to go to prison. "They have sinned!" she shouts. I stand dead still, waiting for her to continue. She suddenly changes her mind, chases the girls out and asks me to sit.

How I dislike these lengthy sessions; the couch at the foot of her bed faces forward so the top half of my body is turned awkwardly towards the princess. Protocol demands – or, more accurately, Mona has told me – that both feet should be on the floor when talking to the princess. After a mere 15 minutes, the contortion makes my back ache.

"I found indecent photos of the staff on their cameras," she says with disgust.

"Indecent, Your Highness?" I ask. "They belong in jail!" she spits out. In one photo, Sunny is posing up against the Amir's Porsche, which incenses the princess. Good God, these women are just trying to inject a bit of fun into their lives. Nothing I hear from the princess even remotely makes me believe they deserve prison.

I find the staff sitting around the basement kitchen table eating lunch. Lilly's eyes are swollen from crying. I put the kettle on and pull out a chair. "What happened this morning?" I ask gently. This prompts more tears from Lilly and she tries to blame it on missing her family. Sunny opens up and I listen with a growing feeling of dismay at what these girls go through.

"The princess found photos on our cameras." I wait for her to continue at her own pace. She gets up and walks to her room to fetch her camera. The first photo horrifies me. Big dark blue bruises the size of the palm of my hand cover Lilly's left thigh. Sunny explains that the princess kicked Lilly and is furious that she has documented the beating. "What are you planning to do with these photos?" the princess screamed. There is another photo that shows distinct finger bruises on Sunny's upper arm where the princess grabbed her and shook her. I am stunned but remain completely calm.

They tell me that in most royal households, after the royals beat a servant, they offer the girls money or jewellery. The amount is dependent on the severity of the beating. If the staff member accepts the offer, the incident is forgiven and not spoken about again.

I ask them if this is the case with them as well. Sunny excuses herself from the table and returns with a large jewellery box filled with cheap trinkets. Each girl has one of these. The evidence of the number of beatings she has received in her thirty months here lies before my eyes.

The two Filipino girls are now crying openly. They take turns telling me their stories. One of the photos the princess is most upset about shows Lilly with a banana in her hand, doubling as a microphone, singing along to the radio as she entertains a group of girls in her home town. This is long before she took up her positions in Saudi. Harmless fun – but the princess believes the photo depicts Sunny simulating oral sex.

So this is why we were locked out. The princess had gone through the girl's computers, cell phones and personal belongings. I know my own bag was searched too but I have no incriminating evidence on me after being warned that the palace is able to intercept text messages and emails. Thank God I took my camera out of my bag before coming to work as it would have revealed our pride in a good batch of pineapple beer documented in photographs.

Then Sunny says something that confirms that I am not losing it. Of 16 PAs in the past five years since the princess moved back home, only one stayed for the duration of her one-year contract and the only reason was that she had nowhere to go. One in 16?! This doesn't make me feel better. Lilly adds that one PA was so desperate to leave that she faked cancer and was sent home on medical grounds.

Another PA faked a sibling's death and got permission to go home for the funeral but never returned.

My contract stipulates that I am only allowed to go home on compassionate leave if a parent or sibling passes away. Both my parents have passed away. I wrack my brains as to which sibling I can kill off but the thought doesn't last long.

Room inspections

☙

IN THE middle of the new week, I arrive at work to screaming from upstairs. A feeling of dread washes over me. The princess had asked the maids to send me up the minute I arrived.

I kick off my shoes before I make my way upstairs. Sunny is standing in front of the princess with her head bowed. She is crying. The princess is furious. She proceeds to tell me what the latest transgression is.

Earlier in the day the princess made a surprise visit to the girl's bedrooms. She found a bowl of sugar in Sunny's room. My instructions are to open their cupboards and throw all their clothes on the floor. Not just Sunny's, all of them. The princess is in such a rage that I dare not say anything but, "Yes, Your Highness."

I gather the girls into the basement kitchen. I don't know whose cupboard to start with. Lilly calls me into her room. Trying to be proactive, she has all her clothes already piled up on the bed. But if the princess suddenly appears behind me to check up, we all go down the Suwanee. Lilly reads my thoughts and throws the clothes on the floor.

Next I go into Mami and Maria's room. They understand that I don't have a choice. I remove piles of folded clothing but instead of throwing them on the floor, I pile the heaps of clothes as neatly as possible on their bedside carpets. These girls have so many items of cheap clothing that their cupboards bulge and to repack it all would be a waste of time.

I try to make it a light-hearted task as I laugh at Sunny's shoe collection. She has about 15 pairs of sneakers, all in different colours, and some with lace or sequins on them. Her sandal collection alone would put Imelda Marcos to shame. She has nowhere to wear them in Riyadh but will have a field day back home.

I go up to the princess to let her know that the task is done. I am told to type out a rules list, have it enlarged and to put one on both of their bedroom doors. I am to do regular room inspections when the girls least expect it.

The list that the princess has prepared for me is ridiculous. I do it anyway. The princess has calmed down and I would like to keep it that way. Tomorrow is Friday and it could not have come sooner. This whole week at work has been tense and I feel completely drained.

The DQ

AS I feel confident that Serge seems to know what he is doing, I allow myself to be persuaded to go out alone with him for the day. I have read so much about the Diplomatic Quarter and today Serge is my guide. He is full of interesting stories and I delight in being the audience instead of problem solver.

The Diplomatic Quarter, or DQ as it is known, is a 1 600 acre walled suburb on the city's western edge and is home to foreign embassies, international organisations as well as residences and malls. Because of this, the DQ is considered a high risk area so getting in is quite a performance.

The entrance is heavily guarded by armed security forces. Serge handles all the questions. He happens to be friends with the Lebanese Consul and uses this to our advantage. After about 30 minutes of formalities, we are allowed in.

I am amazed at the beautiful buildings, tree-lined streets and landscaped gardens. This feels like a different country; it is a haven of tranquillity. A group of girls cycle past the car, laughing and carefree. Cats sit, relaxed, on walls – they have collars and are beloved pets.

On the other side of the boundary wall, a woman walking alone is frowned upon. I miss it, and I feel less fit. Here, women have that freedom. Many lush parks stretch through the residential areas and along the 20km walking track, which follows the perimeter of the DQ. Included are numerous sports facilities, picnic areas, kiddies play parks, courtyards, benches, shaded walkways and private seating areas. It is paradise compared to the world beyond the walls. You could be anywhere in the world.

Each park has a distinct theme, but they are all tranquil with the soothing sound of flowing water from countless fountains, water channels and waterfalls.

Serge points out the various embassies as we drive around. The Australian, British and French embassies throw the best parties, according to Lea. The South African embassy was no slouch either, but now that it is headed by a Muslim man, and alcohol is not allowed, the socials have dried up. Apparently their barbeque evenings were the talk of the expat community.

Eventually we find ourselves near a large square, which has a multitude of restaurants and coffee shops. We take a walk through it, stopping for coffee. After the barrenness of the city on the other side of these walls, I cannot get enough of the beautiful greenery.

Serge asks a teenager skating around with his mates to take a photo of us. We stroll through the myriad walkways and arches. Serge reaches for my hand. For a moment I am taken aback, and look at him, bewildered. Then I relax. His hand is soft and warm. And so is my heart.

Hunger eventually drives us homeward. We decide to stop at a Tamimi's to get a couple of things for an early dinner. We shop like an ordinary couple, a pleasure I have not forgotten though it has been a while. I see the same thought in Serge's smiling eyes as we stand in the queue. I feel his hand find mine for a brief moment between the folds of my abaya.

When we get home, I go to my place first to shower and freshen up before dinner. I walk into a crowded apartment as Mona's Friday guests are still here. I notice the empty bottles of pineapple juice on the kitchen counter. They are all in a boisterous mood. Everyone wants to know what is going on between Serge and me. I pretend to be in a hurry to avoid their questions. A little later I say goodnight to them, as they will have left by the time I return, and escape to Serge's flat. Once again he is waiting for me at the top of the steps.

It is my decision to keep our relationship from the other Lebanese expats in the compound. Every time I leave the flat to go to Serge, I text him to find out if the coast is clear.

Royal wedding

⚜

PRINCESS ISABEL is getting married. There is much excitement at the palace. As tradition dictates, Mona and I are given exquisite pieces of material for our dresses and we are told we may choose our own designs. The material given to me is heavy with crystals and little pearls. On top of that, we are each given money to buy matching accessories like handbags, sandals and costume jewellery.

We organise a visit to the Princess's dressmaker, Madam Lorraine. At her premises on the other side of the city, we go through many international design magazines. In the photos that show spaghetti-strap dresses, the arms are blacked out. I narrow it down to three designs, leaving Madam Lorraine to advise me on the final choice for the elaborate and heavy material.

Despite her limited English, she and I agree on a design and she takes my measurements in a curtained cubicle. One week later, we are called for a last fitting. The dress looks exquisite. Mona and I take samples of our material to shop for accessories. Sultan takes us to a shoe and handbag shop the size of a rugby field. He finds a parking space in the shade and puts his seat down before we are out of the vehicle. There is no rush.

We walk up and down the long aisles, overwhelmed by the variety of styles, until we are both happy with our choices. Next stop, an accessory shop. One whole corner of this large store has shelves from ground to ceiling filled only with tiaras. We are in the Kingdom of Arabia, after all.

Two weeks later, our outfits ready and heady with anticipation, the big day arrives. We are given the day off but have to be at the palace at nine in the evening. Mona is in a good mood and we laugh and joke as we get ready. I feel like Cinderella – though the wedding only starts at midnight. I am at least three inches taller in the stiletto sandals I bought for the wedding. First time in high heels in years. What was I thinking?

There is chaos as we arrive at the palace. Hairdressers, make-up artists and tailors jostle around the royals, pampering them. As I briefly pass my princess in one of the passages in the main palace, she scowls and doesn't return my greeting.

Eventually, at half past eleven, we make our way outside to the fleet of luxury cars. Each driver stands next to his car and waits. Tonight my princess travels with her family and the staff travel separately. For a moment, she stands next to me, and I compliment her on how lovely she looks. She hardly acknowledges me but I know the unspoken apprehension she feels about this wedding.

We arrive at the hotel at midnight. Three thousand guests are invited but as women and men don't mix socially, 1500 women will gather in one hall with 1500 men in another.

The hall is breathtaking – the largest I've ever seen – with trees full of blossoms and fairy lights in keeping with the summer theme. The women's outfits are even more breath-taking. Never have I seen anything as beautiful. Jewels hang like chandeliers from their ears, and are tucked into their hair. Diamonds the size of apricots hang from their necks. Each woman's dress and set of jewels outdoes the next.

The Filipino staff settles in at the back of the hall as Mona and I are shown to our section further to the front. As we take our seats, I see the person who emptied the contents of my purse on day one. I glare at her for the briefest moment before she looks away. I think she got the message that I know it was her. Did I pay for the elaborate dress she is wearing?

Servants dressed uniformly in beautiful tunics and trousers circle the hall with trays of snacks – mostly sweet biscuits and chocolates made from cashew or pistachio nuts, a great favourite in the Middle East. It will keep us going for a while but the nuts have stuck in my teeth and there isn't a toothpick in sight. I don't dare smile at anyone, and try to dislodge the offending particles without looking like a masticating cow.

Several servants spread smoke from incense burners they swing around as they walk. A fog now hangs over everything. Incense is burnt every day in every palace. The women stand in front of the incense burners and fan the smoke into their faces, one going as far as to take the incense holder from a servant to place it under her skirt for a couple of seconds. I watch this through teary eyes – I am not used to the smoke.

Two hours later, the bride still has not made an entrance. It is two in the morning. Mona and I have not moved off our chairs. As exciting as it is watching all the goings on, the fight against nodding off becomes a challenge. Yet this time of the morning is the peak hour for socialising for most Saudis.

The women dance with one another, fully aware that they are being observed in all their splendor. The Arabian music pulses loudly through the hall, making conversation difficult.

I watch my princess as she joins the Amira on the dance floor. I feel so proud of her. She is a vision in her pink floaty designer gown. Her hair is worn swept up with little tendrils hanging down. I know how much looking good for this meant to her; with exercise and a special diet, she had lost about five kilograms. I also know the wedding can't be easy for her.

At quarter to three, everyone takes a seat as the bright lights suddenly dim. All eyes are on the long aisle the bride will walk down to get to the stage where there are seven thrones decorated in fairy lights and flowers. The effect is stunning.

At three, there is a drum roll. Princess Isabel appears in the large doorway that is lit up with blue ultraviolet lights. She stands alone. Her dress is magnificent – a soft blue that shimmers in the light with a train about three metres long. Her hair is swept up, held in place by crystals, with a few curls hanging loose. Suddenly there is a shrill noise as every servant starts ululating.

Princess Isabel takes three steps then stops. She looks from left to right with a serene smile on her face, then after about thirty seconds, takes another three steps and stops. This is repeated as she makes her way to the stage – it takes her an eternity to get there. The bride climbs the stairs and sits on the throne as family and close friends come up to greet her.

The back doors of the hall open to reveal the Amir, Prince Abdullah, Prince Khalid and at last, the groom. The men look straight ahead as they make their way to the stage. Some of the women either cover their faces or turn away as the men pass them. Once on the stage, the men stay for only 30 minutes as the immediate family comes up to congratulate them.

The groom takes his bride's arm and leads her out of the hall. The ululation is deafening. Princess Isabel has four maids carrying her long train as it fans out. She looks so regal until one of the maids accidently steps on her train. The princess turns around and viciously snaps at the poor girl. It is undignified and the onlookers are silent, waiting to see what will happen next. The prince visibly tugs on her arm before the princess turns and proceeds out of the hall. I spot the servant girl who stepped on the train coming back into the hall with red eyes. Did Princess Isabel deal with her once out of the hall? Probably.

For the next two hours, nothing much happens. At five, the guests slowly make their way into the adjoining restaurant. At half past six, we are called in. The restaurant is huge. I have never before seen so much food under one roof; over a hundred different dishes line the periphery of the entire restaurant – and these are just the main courses. Every imaginable dish is there – besides *pap* and *wors*.

The large round dessert table dominates the centre of the restaurant. A two-metre high pyramid of strawberries is surrounded by every desert you can think of.

After an hour, Mona and I make our way back to our seats, refuelled to the brink but dangerously sleepy. The music is still loud, but now, it is grating rather than stimulating. The bridal couple has long since gone so Mona and I hope that the crowd will start thinning. No such luck – the dancing and festivities continue. At half past nine, when I really think I cannot stay awake any longer, my princess calls me over, looking as fresh and lovely as when we left home at midnight. I cannot say the same of myself.

"Mrs C, we are leaving now so after we have gone, you and Mona may go home." I thank her. I am ready to kiss her feet. Just before I turn around, I smile at her and say, "Your Highness, thank you for allowing me to share in this beautiful evening." She smiles broadly.

Mona and I leave the hall in high spirits. The blinding sunlight hits hard. Today is Friday but I can't imagine we will see much of this day. My feet blistered by the high heels, I get out of the car barefoot. My body aches from sitting for so long in a dress that weighs at least 20 kilograms. Once I take it off, I realise quite how cumbersome it is – I feel as if I am levitating. I am asleep before my head hits the pillow, smudged make up and all.

Two days later, Mona and I are getting ready for work when the princess calls Mona. She is outside our compound waiting in the car. She gets off the phone, "For fuck's sakes!" she shouts as she throws her phone down on the couch. "Arabella is outside and she wants to me to go with her to a store but I am not supposed to tell you," she spits out. She is livid, as she has not yet showered and her hair is standing up in spikes. "So why did you tell me?" I ask. She does not respond. My only thought is, "Rather you than me."

The princess arrives back at the villa three hours after I have started my work day. She has no packages, which I find strange. No sooner does she settle in her room when Mona makes an appearance and closes the princess's door after she enters.

I get a text message from the princess to say that I may go. I don't hesitate.

Candlelight dinner and Serge

❧

IT IS Thursday evening and Serge invites me to dinner. After knowing each other for three months, our friendship has progressed into something much deeper. We have become inseparable. Many a night before, I have left Serge's place in the early hours of the morning, but for the first time, I agree to stay over at his flat. The prospect of spending the night with this kind and gentle man and having the whole of the following day together is just too tempting for this mere mortal.

Serge leaves it to me to choose the restaurant. I ask him if we could order in instead. He is happy with the arrangement and refuses any contribution to the meal.

While he goes off to collect our order from a nearby Lebanese restaurant, I take my time preparing. I pack an overnight bag. A small one. Toothbrush, toothpaste, my camera and something to sleep in. It is winter after all. I let myself into Serge's apartment with the key he gave me. He is not back yet.

Radio Nostalgie plays from his computer and for a minute I feel as if I'm in heaven. The most beautiful French ballads enhance the anticipation of the evening. I lie against the soft pillows and duvets scattered on the carpet in the lounge. In the intimate lighting the place looks magical.

At the sound of his key turning in the lock, my stomach twists. He is delighted to see me waiting for him. He hastily puts down the food, falls down onto the carpet and grabs me in a bear hug. We both fall over with the forcefulness of his embrace. "My habibty," he whispers as he releases me slowly, running his hand down the side of my face, looking at me with such love. I don't think I am in heaven any more, I know I am. In Saudi Arabia. Can this really be happening?

The aroma of the food eventually pulls us apart. I had ordered kharouf mashy, melt-in-the-mouth, tender lamb on a bed of rice with roasted cashew nuts.

He jumps up and takes charge. I sit back and watch him. A man who is comfortable in a kitchen will remain an aphrodisiac to my dying day. He lights the candles. After dishing up, he sets the food aside, ready to be served. He produces a bottle of red wine. A gift from a friend in the compound.

On a beautiful ornate gold leaf tray are two exquisitely cut long-stemmed glasses. He hands me my glass. The grapes explode on my tongue as he watches me with pleasure. He stops the music. "I want to play for you a song."

As the first strains of Demis Roussos's 'Quand je t'aime' start playing, he reaches for me and pulls me up. We melt together in a perfect fit. If this is not the most beautiful French song I have ever heard I don't know what is. We slowly move together. The awkwardness I was expecting to feel is not there. Not even a little.

This is seduction at its very best, and in Saudi Arabia, of all places. I did not plan this. In fact romance was the last thing on my mind as I mean no disrespect to the laws of this country or the Koran.

Lea, who has been working in Riyadh for several years and is in a long-term relationship with an American, says relationships in the Middle East take on an intensity like nowhere else on earth – apart from cruise ships, perhaps. Against the backdrop of harsh laws, the relationship becomes your island in a storm.

The fact that Serge and I live in the same compound makes life a lot easier. Suddenly, it feels like coming home. As Serge told me laughingly one night, "the Sahara wind brings love." The sandpit does this to us, but luckily it is not contagious outside its borders.

After a while, Serge seats me back against the pillows and brings over the momentarily forgotten tray of food. It is no longer warm. Though I like my food piping hot, never has anything been so completely unimportant. I love the Lebanese dish, and Serge takes great delight in this. The taste is so heavenly, it makes me miss people I haven't met.

"Please play 'Quand je t'aime' again?" I ask when the dinner is over. I am lying in his arms as he translates the words. I listen to the richness of his voice as he repeats the beautiful lyrics.

'When I love you,
I know the feeling of being a king…'

The world outside ceases to exist. Right now it is just us, in that candlelit room. I give myself over to this sweet man as the Arabian wind blows a gale outside.

Family lunch

❦

I WAKE up the following morning not knowing quite where my limbs start and where his end. I open my eyes to see Serge smiling down at me. He smells so good. We drink our coffee in bed, our talking interrupted with bursts of laughter. What a wonderful way to start the day.

Today I am meeting Serge's family for a traditional Lebanese lunch at his cousin, Mustafa's house. I am excited at the prospect of a day outside the compound with Serge but a low-key nervousness about getting caught stays with me.

Serge holds the car door open as I get into the front seat. As I have been instructed, I drape the hijab over my head as Serge walks around to the driver's seat.

"What you doing?" he asks as he looks at me, his eyes serious. I explain. "No habibty, that is a sure way of drawing the mutawa's attention." I don't understand. He clearly doesn't look like an Arab, so sitting next to a woman who appears to be a Saudi local is bound to draw attention, he says. I remove the hijab and feel surprisingly vulnerable.

It's an amazing feeling, being out of the compound, and sightseeing. Serge is a constant stream of information as we drive through the city. I watch him behind the wheel and feel such a surge of love, I put my hand on his leg as he talks. He squeezes my hand before placing his on the steering wheel again.

I am not always aware of the mutawa's vehicles, but Serge can spot them a mile away. At a busy intersection, Serge gently takes my hand off his leg as we pull up next to a huge 4x4 at the red light. Under his breath, he mutters one word. "Mutawa." I stare straight ahead. It is a tense moment, but they turn right as the light changes to green and I breath out deeply in relief. We laugh at the narrow escape.

Serge tells me that Mustafa's wife is a great cook. She makes the best kibbeh nayyeh, which is the Lebanese version of steak tartar, quite often made from lamb. I am not overly impressed at the idea of raw lamb but I don't say anything. My expression gives me away, though, and Serge laughs.

At the following set of traffic lights, in the car beside ours, I see a sight that chills me to the bone, a boy no older than about 10 behind the steering wheel. He is barely able to see over the dashboard. "What the hell?" I ask Serge. He explains that it is quite accepted and a common sight. Traffic officials turn the other way. And they wonder why the accident rate is so high.

Eventually we stop at a four-storey building. I am a bit apprehensive. The front door opens and Serge hugs the big man standing in the doorway. I am waved in as if they have known me forever. Once inside, we are introduced. The big man is Mustafa. There are two women and three men at the dining room table. The two women get up immediately to make space for us at the table.

Mali, Mustafa's wife, comes over to me with a welcoming smile, and indicates that she would like to take my abaya. She speaks no English but graciously takes the abaya, pulls out a chair for me at the table, then joins the other woman in the open plan lounge, where they sit and watch us.

While the men exchange pleasantries in French, I look around, feeling slightly self conscious. Mustafa walks around the table with two smallish glasses and as he places one in front of Serge, then me, he says, "Arak, good Lebanese drink."

I pick up my glass at the same time as everyone at the table and Mustafa makes a toast "to the woman who has made Serge happy and makes him look 10 years younger". Everyone bursts into raucous laughter as Serge explains to me that at a previous Friday lunch, he had told his cousin about me when he was asked why he was looking so smooth.

Serge is a year younger than me. He likes to keep a week's stubble, but it makes him look much older as his beard is peppered with grey. No one has seen him clean shaven for some time and it really does take 10 years off him.

I take a sip of the arak; the men knock it back in one gulp. It makes my eyes water. I guess it is good if you like aniseed. Next comes a bottle of red wine. Homemade, of course. Again the men make a toast, this time in Arabic. The wine is better than anything I have tasted before.

I catch Serge looking at me with a faraway look in his eyes and it is evident – to me, anyway – that he is reliving last night. I hold his gaze for a while, and what passes wordlessly between us, speaks volumes. We are interrupted by something Mustafa says in Arabic, and everyone laughs.

By this stage I am ravenous. It seems as if everyone has already had lunch as Mali carries the dishes out to the table again. Serge asks if I would like him to dish up for me, which I welcome. Lebanese people are very proud of their cuisine. Their food does not merely satisfy hunger, it is a work of art, reflecting the warm colours of the Lebanese culture.

Spread in front of us is the traditional mezze of falafel, baba ganoush, the ever present tabbouleh salad, chicken kebabs, shish-kebabs, skewered lamb cubes and, of course, kibbeh nay-yeh. After the explanation in the car, I can do without this dish, but Serge tells me I have to at least taste it and adds a small portion to my plate. It is pink in its rawness.

The men at the table keep up a steady stream of conversation, peppered with broken English for my benefit. No one notices as I swallow the kibbeh whole, washed down with the delicious wine. They tell fascinating stories of their home towns in the mountains of Lebanon. We laugh often. How at home I feel among these warm, hospitable people. This is one of the happiest days I have spent in Saudi Arabia.

Early evening, Serge and I say our goodbyes. Mali brings my abaya and helps me as I struggle with the metres of material. She tells Serge to tell me that I am welcome any time. For the first 10 minutes, we drive in a comfortable, happy silence, helped no doubt by the amount of arak and wine we've enjoyed. For once, the roads are quiet.

I ask Serge what Mustafa said when everyone laughed. He smiles and says, "He asked if we want to hire a bedroom." I can't help but laugh. I didn't realise our feelings were that blatant.

We arrive back at the compound and arrange to meet at the pool bar in an hour. I go to feed the cats, which has become a nightly highlight for me. I shake the plastic bowl, which never fails to make them come running. The numbers have doubled – 20 cats at last count. They know me by now and about five of them fight for my affection. Mr Grey has become far more demanding, crawling onto my lap and pushing his little face into my hands. If I had my way, I would take them all home with me.

I have a leisurely shower and pack a bag. Mona like a cat on a hot tin roof, in her efforts to find out why I did not come home last night. What she doesn't know is that I ain't coming home tonight either. Of course she realises I was with Serge but she wants details. Not happening. She invites herself to the pool bar.

Serge is sitting with his group of friends. As we approach, he gets up and pulls out a chair for me. I greet everyone and make a point of greeting Serge as if we haven't seen one another in a while. Unbeknownst to us, we are not fooling anyone – the "pack" has also noticed Serge's happy disposition and youthful transformation.

His attentiveness around the table is a dead giveaway too, as he walks to the counter to place my order for espresso.

He doesn't take his eyes off me and is smiling like an idiot looking for a village. I leave before he does. I have a key to my second home, which beckons like an oasis in the desert. Pun intended!

Our reunion is a joyful one. Serge takes my overnight bag

and puts it in the bedroom. He is in such a good mood, his energy out of proportion with the one-bedroom apartment.

Full of good food, and with an extra bottle of wine as a gift from Mustafa because I raved so much about it, we are both ecstatic at the prospect of the evening together. Serge selects the music then scatters extra pillows on the duvet spread over the soft carpet.

Engelbert Humperdinck is singing "How I Love You" in the background. I can't help thinking that if he'd selected anything by Tom Jones, it would have been the end of this newfound relationship.

In the dim light of the room I look at this man and think, "Where the hell did you come from?" What has transpired is beyond intoxicating – but I am also scared to death. It gives Mona a heap of live ammunition to sink me with.

Buying happiness

❦

THE FOLLOWING day, on my way to the palace, I ask Sultan to stop at a Sugar Sprinkles cake shop. I buy the princess two red velvet cupcakes as she has mentioned to me that cupcakes make her happy, and a chocolate one for each staff member. I need the whole world to be happy today.

I arrive at work, walking on air. My good mood is contagious and soon all the girls are gathered in the kitchen as I catch up with their morning. I try to go through the checklist of daily chores but everyone is laughing and teasing one another. It is such a pleasure to see them like this.

I place the cupcakes on one of the princess's plates and this time, after inspecting it closely for any undesirables, I do add a flower from the garden. I take time folding the paper serviette and place the cutlery inside its folds. Her door is open as I softly knock. Initially, she frowns as I walk in with the tray as she has not asked for anything. But her eyes light up as I place the plate on her bedside table.

"Mrs C, that is beautiful, thank you!". I joke with her as I retreat backwards from the table, "Your Highness, you have been unhappy for a couple of days and as you said that cup-cakes make you happy, I thought I would buy you some extra happiness today." Corny, I know, but it works like magic. She looks at me with a huge smile.

I take this opportunity to give her the flash drive with the documentaries on South Africa. She excitedly accepts and thanks me sincerely. Yes, she is a delight when she is in a good mood.

I smile as I walk out backwards and leave her to it.

"Today we are having a baking lesson," I tell the staff. Teaching the staff to cook and bake is part of my job description so Sunny and I go into the large pantry to select one of the array of baking dishes. Most of the dishes are used regularly and it shows, while all the mod cons in the kitchen on the first floor glisten, untouched. There is an air of excitement as everyone gets involved.

My phone beeps as a text message comes through. I am very happy to read a message from the princess.

My dearest Mrs C, thx so much for this luvly surprise! I know it is a small one but it touched me deeply. J I really appre-ciate everything your doing, I have to admit that I'm really blessed MASHA ALLAH 2 have u as part of my life & as a member of my family as well. ALLAH is always listening 2 our prayers & will always give us & put for us the right ppl in our lives or paths 4 precise reasons. INSHA ALLAH we will have the best times 2gether & 4 a long time. Luv u lots! Xoxo J

Right now, my happiness is complete. Thank you, God, for bringing me to this strange place.

Wednesday night dinners

DEPENDING ON the weather, these dinners for female family members and close women friends who are also part of the extended royal family are either held around the pool or in a purpose-built chalet. The two princes from our palace and the family doctor are the only three men allowed to join the royal women. Oh, and the court jester, a funny little man who seems to be openly gay. For the record, this is only my opinion and not a fact.

Several maids walk around constantly spraying perfume into the night air as the royals hate the smell of food cooking. Whenever Lilly or I cook for the princess, the kitchen door has to be closed. A very strong extractor fan absorbs the delicious aromas.

Tension is building between Mona and me as my princess has instructed me to help out with the Wednesday dinner preparations in the main palace. Mona feels this is her domain, and I am encroaching. When the Amira makes a surprise visit in the kitchen and compliments me on what I am wearing, the look of sheer venom on Mona's face confirms my suspicions: my presence there threatens Mona no end.

The Amira asks me to light the fire inside the chalet, which further infuriates Mona. I don't know why the Amira asked me, but it may be just that I was standing closest to her. I walk in, and without looking at any of the royals seated on the plush couches, some with their feet up, I kneel and start spreading the fire lighters.

I suddenly become aware of a presence behind me and as I turn, I see Mona's furious gaze. She is trying to give the impression that she is supervising me. As the fire jumps into life, I stand up, just to hear Mona thanking me, loudly enough for the Amira to hear. At that moment I feel sorry for her. I excuse myself to go to check on Lilly.

This is the one evening the princess's bedroom, dressing area and bathroom gets an especially thorough clean as the bedroom is vacant for the duration of the dinner, which usually lasts until sunrise. As none of the staff is allowed in the princess's bedroom without rubber gloves, I hastily pull on a pair as I make my way upstairs. Lilly smiles as I enter.

Every second day, Lily brings an out-sized tray down from the laundry with about 30 pillow slips spread out on it for the princess to choose the linen. The collection of bedding is colourful and varied. Once the princess has made her choice, the colour scheme has to match throughout. That goes for towels, bathroom mats, dressing gown, prayer mat and fresh pyjamas put out each day with matching slippers. These items are perfumed every evening. So much perfume is sprayed onto her pillows and sheets that I am not sure how she sleeps with the overwhelming scent.

We are not allowed to touch the princess's phones, not even with gloves on. When the princess asked me to pass her phone, I slipped out a tissue from one of the hundreds of boxes scattered all over the villa, grateful that the staff had shared this detail with me.

I have my own bathroom in the villa. When I first asked the girls for a hand towel, they told me that towels aren't allowed as it is unhygienic, according to the princess. I have to dry my hands on tissues. There are six boxes in my bathroom alone. The tissues may not stick out, but have to be folded over like an envelope on top of the box.

I alternate my evening between supervising the cleaning of the princess's bedroom and the chalet as the royals want us to be visible. A good looking man in his fifties pulls up in a BMW and parks in the middle of the road, next to the chalet. The maids swarm around him. I don't know who he is but he spots me walking past and stretches out his hand. "Here," is all he says as he drops the contents of his closed fist into my hand. I don't look at what he gives me, thinking it is rubbish.

Once back at the villa, I take the crumpled pieces of paper out of my pocket. I am shocked as I look down at SR1500. Just over three thousand rand. Now I understand why the servants of the main palace were all around him – clearly this is not a one-off. He is the Amira's brother.

Mona and I are told we may go at about two in the morning. On the way home, Mona tells me that my princess has a huge crush on this uncle. On their last European trip, my princess made such a nuisance of herself texting the uncle that a family meeting was called in an attempt to dampen her fervour. Apparently Princess Arabella went into isolation after the meeting and did not leave her hotel room to accompany the family on their shopping sprees for four days.

We are both bone eary tired when we get home, so after our nightly ablutions, we hit the sack with minimal conversation. It is easier to go to sleep with soft music playing on my head phones than to listen to Mona's snoring that comes in bursts, like a gatling-gun.

In the morning, I start the DVD inventory. I clear the pile of boxes stacked up against the windows in the basement as

— 185 —

it obscures the natural light coming in from the glass sliding doors that lead to a small patio. There are roughly 20 large boxes of DVDs. I clear a huge area on the immaculate floor and open the first box. It is a fun exercise as I pile them into genres.

The princess has given me permission to help myself to any of her books or DVDs. I come across a movie called "Cairo Time" and after I ask the princess's permission yet again, I take it to watch later. I have the evening to myself as Serge has gone home to Lebanon. It is Christmas Eve.

The compound seems bleak without him.

Christmas Eve

❦

SULTAN STOPS outside the compound and with a heavy heart, I open the gate. Tonight I am missing everybody back home. I bump into Mark as I enter and he insists I join in on the Christmas celebrations in the recreation room downstairs. It is a generous invite and I accept.

First, I feed the cats. I prepare a special meal, soaking pellets with a couple of tins of sardines. The mix stinks as I carry it outside. The cats come running from all directions. I cannot start feeding them until I remove Mr Grey from under my abaya. He is far more interested in the affection he gets than the food.

I stroke the cats that allow me to get close but as usual, Mother Ginger watches from a distance. As I start putting out little heaps of the food, all hell breaks loose. The bigger cats fight viciously for the food so I try to separate them. I scrape the last of the food out and leave them to it.

After changing into jeans, I make my way downstairs to the recreation room. The room is filled with about 30 men, mostly Lebanese, and most from our compound. The smoke of shisha pipes creates a haze over the table. Almost at once, everyone stands up as they greet me. I sit next to Mark, a familiar face. There is one face I miss.

The table is groaning under the weight of the food. Everything you can possibly think of – except pork. Two-litre bottles of 7Up and Pepsi take the place of champagne. The atmosphere is wonderful – everyone seems to be in a good mood, making the most of it, despite not being home for Christmas.

After a couple of tokes from the shisha pipe, Neo starts drumming and the whole room reverberates with the sound of singing. The good will in this room is palpable. I admire the way they make the best of life in Riyadh. Then again, men have so much more freedom than women – most of the guys in the room have their own cars.

Close to midnight, Mona phones me from the flat. She has just arrived home. I invite her to join us, and she walks in to Merry Christmas wishes. This is an ordinary working day for us. We eventually say our goodnights and I thank the guys for their hospitality. Again, I marvel at their impeccable manners.

I lie in bed into the early hours, watching "Cairo Time". It is a poignant movie that breaks my heart a little; it resembles

Serge and my story, and I know the ending. I develop a slight crush on the lead actor who looks a lot like Serge.

Christmas dinner with the royal family

❦

I DON'T know it yet, but we are going out for dinner. It's just as well I made an effort with my outfit as it is Christmas.

I don't wear my daily uniform very often any more as the Amira complained to my princess that my uniforms are terrible and don't look professional. How I love the Amira!

The dinner venue is only about seven blocks away from our palace. Once again, I accompany my princess in her car. The four cars carrying everyone from our palace arrive at the host's gate simultaneously. The gate looks as if it is made of 24-carat gold. It shimmers in the sun, blinding to look at. The gates slip open, a wonderland behind them. Lush vegetation fills the gardens with splashes of colour from real flowers.

We drive past several buildings that make up the entertainment area; each massive hall has its own colour scheme. As we reach the main palace, Sultan opens the door for the princess and I take her abaya and handbag. She joins her family and disappears inside. Mona and I are ushered into the waiting area, a cluster of gold and red couches that are positioned halfway beneath the majestic staircase leading to the first floor.

For a moment I am quiet as I take in the furnishings, artworks, exquisite rugs and chandeliers the size of small swimming pools. The effect is out of this world. The many staff members that scuttle around quietly are dressed in a similar fashion to Air Emirates cabin attendants, except their outfits are gold, with scarves of the lightest cream silk. They look exceptionally well groomed. My own uniforms come to mind.

After two hours of sitting under the staircase with two Lebanese women, PAs from another palace, we are called into one of the many dining halls, a building that stands on its own on the vast palace grounds. Mona and I are both quiet as we take in the splendour.

The dining hall is the size of a rugby field. I feel as if I have walked into a fairytale. The colour scheme is blue and cream, with crystal. A large swimming pool dominates the centre of the room, tiled in nautical patterns in gold and shades of blue. Around the pool are ten 12-seater dining room tables, each different. One that stands out is clear Perspex. Gold candles placed on every surface create a mystical effect.

We are directed towards the buffet, to a cluster of 10 smaller round tables for the staff. Each table has a metre-high vase holding an explosion of colours of flowers. I am fascinating to see that each vase doubles as a fish bowl, in which exotic fish swim in circles.

We are offered a choice of fruit juices by the palace staff while the royals dish up for themselves. Once again, a buffet table about 20 metres long groans with the weight of every imaginable dish. When it is our turn, I fill my plate with prawns. Even though we are in the middle of a desert, these prawns are the best I have ever eaten.

After dessert, we are served Arabian coffee. I have seen ice blocks with little lights in them before, but these brightly lit sugar cubes are new to me. I am not sure if they are edible, so I gently sip my way around them. I ask Mona what would happen if we swallowed them. "Light would shine out of your arse," she says, and we dissolve into giggles. Even Mona has her moments.

Feeding the cats has become a nightly routine and they slowly allow me to get closer to them. Mr Grey goes wild when he sees me and I now spend time sitting on the grass playing with him. He cannot get enough affection. Something black comes hurtling out of the tree; it's a small kitten, just skin and bone, watching the bigger toms warily, after being put in its place once too often.

I gather up some pellets that are still scattered around and slowly fling them towards the black kitten. It lunges forward, grabs a pellet and runs off to eat it. We repeat this a couple of times. What a life these poor animals live. They stand no chance.

Lea has told me, to my horror, that many in Saudi, her palace included, take cats and kittens into the desert, fling them out of the van and drive off, leaving them to die. I feel this cruelty as a physical pain. The desert heat is unbearable, the hot sand blisters bare feet instantly. All I can hope is that they die quickly.

Second visit to Doctor Friendly

❦

THREE MONTHS after my arrival in Saudi, I wake up on a Saturday morning with a feeling of inexplicable dread. I feel burnt out. I am teary and shaking; tension overwhelms me. I cannot face going into work today. Although I try to talk myself into it, I can't. The only way to get out of work is to go to the doctor. Physically there is nothing wrong with me.

I fluctuate between overwhelming relief when I get home after a day at the palace and acute apprehension on my way to work. Whether it will be a good day or a day from hell depends on the princess's mood. These people wield real power. If a royal killed a staff member, it would be swept under the carpet, never to be mentioned again.

After phoning the princess who shows concern and assures me that she will send a driver straight away, I shower and am ready in no time. On the way to the hospital, the princess phones and asks me to come by the palace after my doctors visit, not to work, just to make sure I am okay. How do I tell her that she is the cause of my severely unsettled mental state?

— 194 —

I cannot quite believe that Dr Friendly, after asking me where I am from as if he has never seen me before, goes through the whole "Goeiemôre, hoe gaan dit?" spiel again. I understand that he sees a lot of patients, but still. He accompanies me to his consulting room and closes the door behind us.

As much as I try to contain myself, I cannot stop the tears. I am not openly sobbing but the tears just keep on coming. A constant stream of medical personnel interrupts us, even though the door is closed. I am a mess but the intruders pretend not to notice and I am too exhausted to care if they do.

Between the ongoing interruptions, I try to tell him how unhappy I am, not because of Riyadh itself but because of the person I am working for. He asks me why I don't leave. I tell him why I can't. If I break my contract before the year is up, I have to pay a $4000 penalty to the princess, my ticket back home and the recruiter's fee for the remainder of the contract, which is 25% of my annual salary. The amount is close to R90 000. I feel trapped. There is no way I can manage that.

I think back to all the goodbye parties back home where male friends jokingly promised that should I be unable to leave Saudi, they would find a way to get me out. Their promises seem absurd now, but I loved them for saying so.

I ask the doctor's advice. I plead with him, not quite sure

how he can help me. He listens, concerned. The tears refuse to stop. I tell him of the constant tension, of the princess's terrible moods and bullying demands and I touch on the subject of the abuse she metes out, now almost daily.

In my desperation, I ask him if he could send me home on medical grounds. He acts as if he doesn't know what I'm talking about. Perhaps SR30 000 would refresh his memory but I don't have it anyway.

After our talk, he is kindness itself and instructs a waiting nurse to take my blood pressure and to draw blood. Alarm bells go off as I am convinced the blood tests will reveal the red wine from the previous day. "When will you have the results of the tests, Doctor?" I ask, innocently. "In about a week," is his reply. Okay – so for a week my flesh will remain intact and I can still enjoy the sanctity of my own bed.

Sultan is waiting outside and we make our way to the palace. I have hardly entered the villa when the princess comes flying down the stairs to the entrance level. She is pale and for a reason I am yet unaware of, she is livid.

Dr Friendly phoned her soon after I left his rooms and repeated almost everything I told him. I was expecting sympathy.

She is outraged that I had the audacity to discuss my work conditions with the doctor. "Pay your penalty and you can go!"

she shouts. Although prayers blare from the little radio on the windowsill, they don't drown out the princess's harsh words.

I am learning the hard way that the protocols and work ethics of the Western world mean nothing in Saudi Arabia. Doctor-patient confidentiality doesn't seem to exist. I am stunned. In reaching for help, I put the first nail in my coffin.

The friendly doctor advised her that it would be better to let me go. "Why keep someone who doesn't want to be here? It is counterproductive," he said. At least that showed some sound judgment. I realise nothing I can say will aid me so I stand in front of her with my hands behind my back as protocol demands and I don't say a word. She rants for what feels like an eternity. As beautiful as she is when she is in a pleasant mood, she is ugly, with veins bulging on her forehead, when she is angry.

I look up at her contorted face now and again, but mostly keep my eyes down in an effort to defuse my simmering anger at the injustice of it all. I am angry that anyone, especially one so young, so unimportant in the bigger scheme of things, has the power to abuse others so.

My face betrays none of these thoughts. When she's had her fill, she dismisses me. With a "Thank you, Your Highness," I turn and walk out of the room, breaking protocol. It is not intentional but I am not thinking straight. I make my way to the front gate where Sultan is waiting to take me home.

Holding my head in my hands so that Sultan cannot see my tears, we drive to the compound. I have reached one of the lowest points in my life.

As we pull up to the compound gates, Sultan turns in his seat and offers me a chocolate with a slight smile. This has never happened before. I don't think this gentle man will ever know what his gesture of kindness meant to me. In a way, it was an outstretched hand of unity. He has felt the same despair. We are in the same boat. To this day I have not forgotten the feeling of utter amazement that kindness does still exist in a moment when I felt most alone in the world.

No doubt, the worst is still to come.

I arrive back at the compound and go straight to Serge's apartment. The kettle is on and he is waiting for me. The pillows and duvet on the carpet have been straightened in anticipation of my arrival. After kicking off my shoes, I fall down onto the pillows. I am too drained to talk much. He leaves me on my own. After a while, he puts the ornate gold leaf tray down in front of me. He pulls me into his arms and gently rocks me. It is surprisingly soothing. We sit like this for a few minutes, not talking, and it calms me completely.

I start to talk, my face half buried in his neck as his arms are still wrapped around me. I tell him about what I saw as the doctor's betrayal. He vehemently tells me not to trust anyone, ever! He is visibly upset and I end up comforting him. Under his breath, he mutters, "Fucker," as he stares menacingly into the air. I explode with laughter as I have never heard Serge swear. Maybe it was the intensity of his statement, but I feel better for it.

"Habibty, listen to me," Serge says as he moves around to face me. "Move in with me," he says simply. At my silence, he repeats what he has just said. I love him for it, but it is impossible. I would not put it past the princess to make an impromptu visit to our compound.

Some evenings at home, I switch my phone off. If the princess doesn't reach me, she contacts me on Mona's phone. And when she does reach me, she asks to speak to Mona immediately afterwards. If I was with Serge and the princess asked to speak to Mona, I would have to run up a flight of stairs and down the passage to our flat. It is just too much of a risk. I tell him so.

I am too distracted to stay over. He understands, but asks me if he could stay over at my place. I cannot help but laugh at his earnest face. Mona would have a field day with this – having another guest in "her" apartment. I beg off, saying I am exhausted and not good company. He walks me up the stairs.

— 199 —

Dreaded confrontation

❦

SULTAN IS waiting for me at the gate at two the following day. The trip to the palace is far too short. I kick my shoes off as I enter the villa. The staff heard every word the princess shouted at me the day before and respectfully avoid eye contact. They seem gentler than before.

"Madam, we kept you some cake," says Maria as I walk into the kitchen. My fondness and respect for these women grows with each day. Here I am, much older, supposedly wiser, yet they seem to handle the princess better than I do. They are so sweet and accepting of the almost daily abuse. Because of this, I feel protective of them and this fuels my resentment towards the princess. I understand that she is hurting but how do I show her that relief does not come this way?

She eventually calls for me. I am not invited to sit. "Good afternoon, Princess," I greet her softly. "You will call me Your Highness!" she responds sharply, glaring at me. Without hesitation, I repeat, "Yes, Your Highness." She is scowling. For the first time ever, I feel a strong dislike for this slip of a girl who believes she is superior to the rest of mankind – by accident of birth.

She does absolutely nothing all day except shout down – rather than phoning – to the basement whenever she wants something. Whenever she wants me, she shouts for one of the girls, who rush upstairs, only to be told to call Mrs C.

As I stand in front of her, I have had about as much as I can take.

Anger has replaced the overwhelming fear I have felt over the last 24 hours, knowing this confrontation was looming. I've reached the point of not caring what happens, which is dangerous for me. For now, I am still going along with protocol and just basic good manners. It doesn't last long.

"What is wrong with you?" she shouts. "Your Highness, if you feel that there is so much wrong with me, I suggest I phone Mr Lewis to send a replacement." My reply leaves her looking at me in disbelief as I have never spoken back to her. "Mr Lewis!" she screams. "He doesn't give a fuck about you!" Did the princess who is perfection herself, in her eyes at least, just use the word "fuck"? I almost want to laugh, the tension is so thick.

"I beg to differ, Your Highness," I respond rebelliously.

She takes a deep breath before continuing in a harsh voice,

"The only time Mr Lewis contacted me was via email on the second day after you arrived for full payment. Not once have they phoned to see how you are doing and still you protect them?!"

I keep quiet. What can I say to that? Although Mona has warned me on many occasions that the princess lies incessantly, I don't know what to believe. And I don't trust what Mona tells me either.

She changes topic. "The doctor told me everything you said to him. How dare you discuss your work conditions, how dare you!" she screams. I know the doctor spoke to the princess but I also know that he could not have told her everything otherwise I would have been in shackles by now. "Who am I supposed to speak to if I cannot speak to a doctor, Your Highness?" I am still bristling at how little doctor-patient confidentiality means here.

"You have attitude, and Mrs M thinks so as well!" she shouts. I could see this coming. All those evenings behind closed doors, Mona was trying to integrate herself into our villa. Mona's job is not secure and her contract is about to come to an end. She has often come home in tears, complaining that her staff won't listen to her. Lately, she has taken to buying my staff little gifts – chocolates and useless trinkets.

"You are a butler! You shouldn't have any emotions!" the princess rants.

By now, it is obvious to her that I am angry. Though protocol demands that my hands remain behind my back, I am waving them around in emphasis as I try to make my point. I shoot back, "Yes, that is true, but I am a human being first, Your Highness."

Before I can carry on, she screams, "I have watched *Downton Abbey* and you are nothing like that butler!" Did I just hear her correctly? I want to tell her that if she was anything like those employers, I could also serenely go about my daily tasks without any emotion but I know the thought would be wasted on her so I say nothing.

"No one has EVER spoken to me the way you speak to me," she screams. Without hesitation, I shoot back, "Well, Your Highness, then we have something in common. No one has ever spoken to me the way you speak to me either!"

I know I have just sealed my fate, but I feel it had to be said. Not that I planned it; it was out of my mouth before I could give it any thought. And I had pointed at her when I said it. A grave mistake.

"Get out! Get out! Get out!" she screams. I turn around on the spot and walk out.

Thirty minutes later, switchboard calls to tell me the driver is waiting for me. The princess's door is closed but I text her goodnight anyway. Surprisingly, she replies with a curt goodnight.

I ditch the abaya as soon as I get home and join the guys at the pool. I need the distraction tonight as my mind is racing. Mona arrives home an hour later and joins us outside. Quite clearly she knows what went down at the villa. The conversation turns to work.

"I am highly respected by my staff," Mona lies blatantly, without blinking. I just look at her. Dislike for her grows by the minute. I came outside to get away from the turmoil at the palace, not to listen to Mona polishing her own marble.

Serge listens to this as he is the only one at the table who knows what is going on. As we make eye contact, I give a slight nod that only he sees and he knows it means it is time to go. He winks at me in understanding.

I say goodnight to everyone and get up to leave. Mona has not finished her coffee and looks at me in surprise as if she expects me to wait for her. This is one evening I cannot stand the sight of her. I don't even look in her direction as I walk away from the table and am out of the flat before she has a chance to return.

Psychiatric evaluation

❦

THE FOLLOWING day I am told by Lilly that the princess wants to see me as soon as I get in.

"Doctor wants to see you again," the princess spits out at me. My mouth is bone dry when I ask the princess why he wants to see me. She ignores my question. I have learned that this is when the princess comes alive. She thrives on drama as this makes her own life more exciting. "Your appointment is in one hour. Sultan will take you." Before I can say anything, she says loudly, "You are dismissed!"

I am royally pissed off that I have to face this doctor, when he has betrayed my confidence. How will I manage to be civil to him?

An hour later, we are at the hospital. This time round there is no "Hoe gaan dit?" from Dr Friendly. From now on, I'm calling him Dr Traitor. There is little by way of greeting from me either.

I sit opposite him, the wide desk separating us. My face is blank and I say nothing. He is sweetness itself. He speaks to me as if I have a mental disorder and need to be treated with kid gloves. "Mrs C, in order to help you, would you consider going to a doctor friend of mine?" I want to laugh at the question that is not a question at all. I know this has come straight from the princess.

Between the two of them, they have decided to send me for a psychiatric evaluation.

Most of the royal family in Saudi live for their sessions at psychiatrists. Is there room for pity here? These privileged people travel the world in private jets, have more food than they need, and live in lavish palaces with staff catering to their every whim.

I am, in my opinion, of sound mind and have nothing to hide so I agree to go. Not that I have a choice – my appointment has already been made. Doctor Traitor assures me that he will chat to the psychiatrist to brief him.

On what? That there is an expat on the loose who does not take kindly to abuse?

At six that evening, Sultan drops me in front of the huge hospital. After inquiring at three different counters, I am sent to the other side of the huge hall where the psychiatry department is situated. The waiting hall is packed.

The receptionists look at me as if I have just wandered in

off the street looking for trouble. The doctor is fully booked and cannot see me, they say. I tell them that I have an appointment but it has been overlooked in the frenzy of this busy hospital. Then I add that my employer, a princess, made the appointment. There is a sudden change in attitude, and half an hour later, I am called in.

The doctor has squeezed me into his full schedule. He remains seated when I walk in. He is a bear of a man. The harsh neon lights reflect off his bald head. He introduces himself and immediately asks "What can I do for you?" in a raspy voice with a thick accent – not local – that I don't recognise. He is evidently annoyed that my intrusion will make him run late.

"I don't know," I say. "Did Dr Traitor not speak to you?" He looks at me blankly. I can't help thinking that he looks more in need of treatment than I do. I explain that between my employer and her doctor, it was decided that I am in need of help. He phones Dr Traitor. After a five minute conversation, he puts the phone down and looks at me as if he doesn't know where to start.

Well, I do.

"Doctor, how do I know I can trust you?" He looks a bit bewildered at my question but before he can respond, I tell him of the betrayal I experienced at the hands of the family doctor. He sits very still as I explain what has transpired, to bring me to his rooms. He tells me that this is to be expected from a doctor who works in the emergency section of a hospital but assures me that what we speak about will remain confidential.

I wish I could make his night by telling him something profound but all I can offer is, "My employer and I had an argument, Doctor. It happens every day all over the world. But does it call for a psychiatric evaluation?"

I am very careful about what I say to him in case it gets repeated again and I find myself in handcuffs. The royal family own Saudi Arabia. They are not only above the law, they are the law. I make a point of not getting too excited, keeping my voice neutral and speaking in a well modulated tone as I relay a little of what went down – I don't want to be diagnosed with some manic mental disorder. He nods as he listens, it plays havoc with the light beams reflecting off his sweaty head.

What he tells me next has me sitting on the edge of my chair. "In Saudi Arabia, you must trust no one!" He says this with an urgency that commands my full attention. "Even Arabs who are best friends know better than to trust their brothers sitting at the table next to them."

What a sad way to live, I think. I don't voice my thoughts, though, as this is an interesting comment, especially from a professional, and as such, I take note.

Again he repeats, "Don't ever trust anyone in this place!" I take it he means in Saudi, not the hospital. "Be very aware of the staff you have to manage as they will betray you in a moment if they think it will better their lives." I am about to say that the staff I work with would never betray me but the good doctor is on a roll. "Be especially careful if you are sharing accommodation with another expat; never ever trust them."

I ask him why he feels that no one can be trusted. "At the end of the day, it is every man for himself in this country." Now it is my turn to nod.

"Never show your intelligence to any member of the royal family as they all suffer from inferiority complexes." He continues as I clamp my dropped jaw shut. "Even if you come up with good ideas, always let them think it was their idea as their low self esteem will not tolerate your intelligence."

I cannot believe what I am hearing. Surely this man must know that criticising the royal family is punishable by death?

The hour passes quickly. As I am about to take my leave, the doctor hands me a prescription. I accept it with an obvious question mark worked into the frown on my face, but before I can ask what it is for, the doctor stands up, takes my hand and tells me the pills are mild relaxants for the times when life in Riyadh becomes too stressful. "They will not harm you, Mrs Garcia, they can only help." The prescription is for 10 tablets only. I am not above being helped, so after thanking him, I make my way to the hospital's pharmacy, the only place that the script can be redeemed.

On the way home, I ask Sultan to stop at Tamimi's. Generally the drivers are happy to oblige as we buy them a two litre Pepsi or some chocolates every now and then.

I join the crowd of men standing at the cake counter. I am almost at the front when a teenage boy shoves me to the side and cuts in front of me. I have never had patience with people cutting into queues but on this day a blinding anger grips me, and with a sideways thrust of my hip, I shove the youngster about two metres back. With that momentum, he almost knocks over the two men standing behind him. Everything stops as the youngster and I glare at one another – never mind the hostile stares I'm getting from the other male shoppers. The man behind the counter wisely serves me immediately, no doubt to avoid further confrontation.

When I get home, I phone Mr Van Wyk, of the Academy. He listens with growing alarm; they don't have an inkling as to how I am faring. He is appalled at what I tell him and suggests that they could intervene to get me home, if I wish. I tell him that I would like a chance to fix it myself, and ask him not to do anything for now. It is immensely comforting to know that he believes what I have told him, and is prepared to take a stand.

The following morning I am so tense at the thought of going to work that I take one of the tablets the doctor has given me. Thirty minutes later I am floating six inches off the floor as I make my way outside to the waiting driver. I am mesmerised by the hustle and bustle around me as I feel somehow detached from it all. The Arabic prayers on the car radio sound beautiful and I ask Sultan to turn it up. I do not miss his surprised look in the rear view mirror. He smiles as he ups the volume.

Surprisingly, the princess is calm as we face each other. If I was any calmer, I'd be in a coma, thanks to the little pink tablet. The psychiatrist has evidently given her a good report. "Mrs C, I have spoken to the doctor. If you really don't want to be here, you can go home without paying the penalty."

"Your Highness, I would like to make a suggestion; let's try for another month. If it doesn't work after that, we can annul the contract." Strangely, she seems pleased with my suggestion, and agrees to it.

She asks me to close her door as I leave her room. My day goes on pretty much as normal. I don't see the princess as she sleeps for the rest of the day. At ten, I get a call from switchboard. My chariot awaits. I am so relieved that the terrible tension of the last few days is over, it's as if a huge weight has been lifted off me.

I sleep well that night, despite Mona's snoring.

Punishment time again

❧

THE FOLLOWING morning, I feel refreshed. I am champing at the bit, and I go to work with a light heart. The minute I step into the villa, Lilly tells me the princess wants to see me.

I knock softly and make sure I have a smile on my face as I greet her. She does not return my greeting. "You need to punish Sunny!" she says harshly. I wait for her to continue. "How dare she inconvenience me?" she rants. "A month ago, Lilly asked me if she could send her boxes home. This morning, Sunny comes and asks me. How dare she?"

I don't see where the princess is going with this. The shipping company had been called to collect Lilly's boxes that afternoon anyway; what difference would it make to collect four boxes instead of two? The girls pay to send the boxes home themselves and it is not as if the princess has to pack them.

I stand there with a blank look on my face. Mona has warned me that the princess hates it when she cannot read your facial expressions. I have found that this is true.

"You will go downstairs and shout at Sunny so loud, I want to hear you from up here." She says this with a smug smile as if she is chuffed with the punishment she has come up with.

"Your Highness, I have never had to raise my voice at any of my staff. Please will you trust me to handle this?" I ask her. "You will follow orders!" she screams at me. I back out with a "Yes, Your Highness" and go downstairs where Sunny and Lilly are polishing the wooden banister on the first floor. They heard the orders and with a nod of my head, I beckon them into the basement. They follow soundlessly on their stokkinged feet.

Sunny stands in front of me, eyes rimmed red from crying. Lilly looks downwards. I understand Sunny's distress; the boxes take six weeks to reach their destination and it is not clear when the princess will give her permission to send more home.

"You heard the princess, Sunny. I have a problem with this as I don't believe you deserve it," I say gently. Lilly looks up and whispers, "Just do it madam." I look at Sunny. She nods and repeats, "You have to do it, Madam."

I take an exaggerated breath and start. "Sunny!" I shout. The girls start giggling as they see me struggle to find the right words. "What were you thinking, inconveniencing the princess like this?" The girls are now doubled over and I hear chortling coming from the kitchen where Maria and Mami are trying hard to mind their own business. I can't help smiling as I continue just a little longer. The princess would want her money's worth. "What would you do differently next time?" I shout.

I hate myself for this; it feels stupid and primitive. Sobering up, Sunny mutters that she would ask the princess's permission a month before the time. I still don't get what the fuss is about as the transport company collects at an hour's notice, anywhere in Riyadh.

So much for thinking things would improve after the agreement the day before.

Another showdown

⚜

WE HAVE a regular visitor, a beautiful cat that lives a couple of doors down. She regularly scratches at our door when she wants to be let in. Mona, who is also a cat lover, welcomes these visits from this affectionate cat.

One morning, I hear the usual scratching, and open the door. The cat shoots past my legs and heads straight for the couch. Mona barrels out of her bedroom and demands that I throw the cat out. She is in a foul mood. Without a word, I pick up the cat and gently deposit her outside the door before turning on Mona.

"What the fuck is your problem?" I shout at her. Everything I had managed to keep to myself up to now, spews out with a fury that leaves me short of breath. I am shocked at the extent of my anger.

Recently Mona has taken it upon herself to advise me on how to handle Princess Arabella. But her own fears taint the advice, which is not always to my benefit. I get the feeling she is deliberately setting me up. As if life here were not hard enough, I end up sharing with someone whose insecurities make for a very devious person!

In front of the compound crowd, she puts on a tough exterior, advising me to treat my princess like the "spoilt three-year-old child she is". "Just throw in a couple of 'Insha'Allahs' and you should be fine," she reckons. Her boldness in front of the intrigued audience amazes me as her interactions with my princess drip with sweetness. The psychiatrist's words echo in my mind, "Trust no one!" This goes against my nature, though, to my detriment at times.

Months of frustration at being told what to do, how to do it and when to do it, burst out.

Mona retaliates with as much vigour. Her festering issue is that she has a sense of ownership of the apartment, after having it all to herself for nine months. I have always bristled at being treated as a guest in what is just as much my home, but till now I have kept it to myself.

I cannot believe what has been eating at her for so long. "There were no kitchen utensils when I moved in. I bought everything with my own money, just to have you waltzing in and using all my stuff!" she rants. I ask her if she would prefer me to double up on everything so that she could have her toaster and kettle all to herself.

— 217 —

Mona is also very angry that we earn the same salary. She sees herself as the Major Domo and me, a mere greenie out of butler school – her words.

Initially I stare at her, then start laughing. "Major Domo, you reckon?" The argument that ensues lasts for about an hour. We are both exhausted afterwards.

Witchcraft

❧

THERE IS something brewing at the palace that is making me very uncomfortable. For three nights now, Mona has been in the princess's room, behind closed doors, for hours on end. I have experienced her forked tongue all too often, so I know she is feeding the princess subtle lies to enhance her own position.

Oh Mona, don't you know that you cannot make your own light shine brighter by extinguishing someone else's.

As I get to the basement, Lilly tells me that I am not allowed into the kitchen. I have to get my laptop, which is charging next to the microwave, so I go in. The strangest looking man is stirring the contents of a pot so big it takes up the entire surface of the stove.

He looks surprised, but says nothing. I glance into the pot from where I am standing. It is filled to the brim with a muddy liquid, and what looks like berries and herbs float in it.

Once back in the lounge area, I ask Lilly what the hell is going on. She says one word that chills me to the bone.

"Witchcraft." I refuse to let it go, following her into her bedroom. "Lilly, speak to me!" I implore.

"Madam, starting tomorrow, for three days we have to spray every inch of the villa and palace grounds with this liquid to chase away evil spirits." I see several plastic spray bottles at the ready in the lounge. The princess has not mentioned a word of this to me. I hear from Lilly that she has put Mona in charge of the operation.

An hour later, I get a call from the switchboard to let me know that my driver is waiting to take me home, at the princess's order.

Whenever I do not get the chance to say goodnight to the princess in person, I text her goodnight. Tonight I don't.

Mona stays behind as Sultan takes me home. I go straight to Serge's flat. It is so good to have someone I can speak to and trust, despite what the doctor says. Serge is a good listener and as he has lived in Riyadh for so long, I heed any advice he gives me. He gets up, fetches something in the bedroom and returns with a serious look on his face.

"Habibty, give me your hand," he says softly. The look in his eyes brooks no argument. Without hesitation, I slip my hand into his. I watch as he gently turns my palm upwards and transfers what is in his hand. A petite wooden rosary with a wooden cross on the clasp. I absorb the message before he says, "Take this with you, my love. It will protect you."

Our eyes sear into one another's when they meet. This could get me beheaded. I am torn between prison or hell. I take the rosary.

I go back to my flat at about one in the morning to shower and change. Mona is sitting at the kitchen table. She is in a talkative mood. I am not, as I know that the truth and what she tells me are sometimes far apart.

As I pack an overnight bag, she tells me she is afraid of what she has to do the next day. With three of my staff, Mona has to spray the premises. She has prayed hard about it and believes God will protect her. "Well, then you have nothing to worry about," I tell her glibly as I say goodnight and close the front door behind me.

The devil's business

❧

WE ARE collected for work at twelve. Mona bypasses her palace as she walks down to the villa with me. I excuse myself to go down to the basement; Mona goes upstairs to the princess's room.

There is hardly any space on the kitchen table as the girls are busy decanting the foul smelling liquid into the plastic bottles. I stick my hand into my trouser pocket to feel for the wooden rosary.

Mona comes into the kitchen to collect the girls. Armed with two bottles each, they leave to start from the corner of the palace grounds. Two hours later, Mona comes in and complains about severe backache. "This is Devil's business," she says with disgust. I pretty much ignore her as I stare at my laptop screen, my focus firmly on the recipe book I have started for the princess.

At ten, I get a text message from the princess to say that I may go. Mona is livid that it does not include her. My heart breaks for her.

Day two of the spraying starts off really badly. The princess is in a thunderous mood. I try to stay out of her way as I hear her shouting at someone on the phone. An hour later I hear blood curdling screams coming from the princess's room. I don't move from the basement.

Today is Wednesday and the usual dinner gathering starts at about ten.

As soon as the princess leaves to join her family in the chalet, I rush upstairs to help Lilly clean up the princess's room. I come to an abrupt stop when I enter. The carpet is soaked with the foul liquid and all the herbs and berries are lying scattered on top of it.

There is a kiddie's blow-up pool in the dressing room with an inch of the muddy liquid at the bottom. It seems the liquid was poured over the princess as well. My skin prickles as I feel for the wooden rosary in my pocket again. Lilly is working furiously.

With a scoop and brush, we work silently on all fours. I start at the far side of the room. One hour later, we have removed most of the mess but have not quite finished when the princess storms in unexpectedly. Her mood has deteriorated even further.

"Why aren't you finished?" she screams at Lilly. Before

Lilly can answer, she yells in an even louder voice, "And why is she helping you?" pointing at me. Lilly does not say a word.

Her arm is already up to protect herself as the princess sweeps past her. Lilly, still sitting on her haunches, slams into the wall as the princess shoves her with her knee. She screams at me to get out of the room. I leave, but stay just outside the double wooden doors. God help me, tonight I will not let her mete out another beating.

The screaming continues for about 10 minutes with sporadic apologies from Lilly. My body is rigid with tension as I listen to the princess call Lilly every derogatory name in the book. Then the princess decides on Lilly's punishment.

"You will go downstairs and fill a bucket with ice and water. I am going to pour it over your head and you will stand like that the whole night."

The next sentence is screamed with full force, "And that South African can go home if she doesn't like it!"

I almost bump into Lilly hurrying from the room as I enter. "You are right, I don't like it, Princess, so maybe it is time for me to go home." I am angry but manage to say the words in a normal voice. I turn around without waiting to be dismissed and go down to the basement where Lilly is busy emptying all the ice trays from all the fridges into a bucket.

"Lilly, will the princess really do this?" I ask. Lilly does not reply or even look up from her task. She has a sickening yellow pallor to her.

Ten minutes later Sunny comes to me to say that the princess wants my iqama. There can only be one reason for this – to obtain an exit visa. As I hand over my iqama to Sunny, she says softly, "The princess said you can go home." I look over at Lilly but she does not look up.

I gather my belongings and just before I slip my abaya over my head, I take another one of the tablets the doctor gave me. My gut is tied in knots. I am asleep on the back seat of the car before we reach the compound.

I briefly stop at Serge's flat but I am so tense and bone weary tired, I don't even stay for tea. His concern endears him to me even more but at the end of the day, I stand alone.

I sit in the stillness of our flat. Mona is not home yet. My brain races with thoughts and words still left unsaid. In the semi darkness, I pick up a pen as I reach for relief. The words spill out of me.

WHERE TO FROM HERE?
I am broken in – so where to from here
Disbelief reigns within the mist – of a debilitating fear

Knee-capped by the blow – my head on the concrete floor

I besiege with a savage cry – Lord show me an open door

A primal scream – from depths unknown

No one to hear – my anguished groan

Another test of endurance – another bitter pill

Is this the lowest pit of darkness – my soul was sent to fill?

I beg to know how long my due – and am waiting for
instruction

The lesson is the easy part – the wait, my soul's destruction

The following day, Sultan collects me at four. I make my way downstairs to the basement where I find Lilly with eyes so severely swollen from crying, she can hardly see out of them. "Lilly, did the princess really do this?" I ask urgently. Lilly still does not respond.

Sunny comes into the kitchen and tells me the princess wants to see me. I have decided on a change of tactics as I have come to realise that trying to reason with the princess is a losing battle. I will not say anything. No matter what she throws at me, I will not speak.

I knock and enter. I have not even come to a proper stop yet when she starts. I keep my face completely expressionless as I focus my gaze on her with an unwavering look. It is driving her mad that I'm not responding.

"You are weak!" she screams, trying to provoke me into saying something. All I repeat is, "Yes, Your Highness." Eventually she runs out of things to say so she starts repeating herself. "You are so weak, I am half your age and I am so much stronger than you!" All she gets from me is a slight smile that probably looks more like a sneer and the repeated, "Yes, Your Highness."

I am not sure when she realises that this is going nowhere. Her face is puce from all the screaming. We end the evening glaring at each other for what feels like an eternity. "You're dismissed," she says calmly. I give a brief nod, release my hands from behind my back and wish her a good night. After walking five steps back, I turn and leave the room.

As I get my things together, the phone rings and the switchboard alerts me that Sultan is waiting. The drive home feels surreal.

I briefly stop in at Serge's apartment. He repeatedly asks me to stay. I beg off. I desperately need solitude to try to work through what happened in the last two days.

The first grains of the sandstorm hit. It is my first experience of one. I'm feeling a little nervous, so I consider staying with Serge. Common sense wins and I find myself eating grit as Serge runs me to my door.

— 227 —

Mona is not home yet as I slip into bed. The noise from outside is scary. As tired as I am, my brain is far too active to fall asleep. Two o'clock finds me in bed with a book when there is a knock at my bedroom door. Mona delivers the envelope.

Last night

❧

I RUN two doors down into a wall of sand, to what has become my island in a storm.

He starts laughing happily as he opens the door for me, thinking I have changed my mind about staying over. I draw him down onto the duvet that now has become a permanent feature on our magic carpet and he immediately senses something is wrong before I start to speak. He doesn't interrupt me once.

We agree to stay awake and treasure the time left together. For a moment, at a loss for words, Serge shakes his head and pulls me into an urgent kiss. He pulls away as abruptly. I can see he is grappling with something but I am totally unprepared when he asks me to join him in Lebanon. Apparently that is accepted by the church, but divorce is not? I listen as he maps out his plan.

He will move back to Lebanon, and continue with architecture but open a business on the side. We will get an apartment and live together. I watch him sketch this lovely picture and my love for him swells as he makes it sounds so easy and uncomplicated. I know it is far from it. There is a small part of me that is momentarily tempted when I contemplate this wild adventure, but I softly tell him that I cannot do it.

The whole world seems to accept that he is separated, and even his immediate family has made peace with it. But I cannot see myself living in Lebanon under these circumstances – also, our cultures are just too different. All the changes that will have to take place for us to be together will have to be made by me.

I invite him to South Africa. He listens intently when I again tell him about Cape Town, the freedom, the spectacular beauty and, of course, the good wines. He holds me the whole time. Nothing is really resolved but the invite to South Africa is an open one. No expiry dates.

He suddenly gets up to fetch something from the bedroom. "Habibty, keep this for me until I come and claim it back," he says as he hands me the crystal rosary. My heart feels as if it's going to burst with love for him.

Serge has been nothing but a pillar of strength. Although we've known each other for the four months I've been in Riyadh, we have only been together for one month.

I open my purse and take out the key Serge gave me to his

apartment. He looks at it in my outstretched hand and gently closes my hand with his. "No. Keep it, my love, and know you will always have a home in Riyadh."

I feel the tears prickling but manage to hide it in the long embrace that follows. I am Princess Sahara after all. If only in his eyes.

The final goodbye

I STACK the last of my luggage at the front door. Mona says a teary goodbye and hugs me.

What a hypocrite she is. Mona has been trying to convince the princess that she could run the main palace and her villa for half of my salary added to hers. That explains the clandestine meetings behind closed door those many nights, and the overt attempts at winning over my villa's staff.

I leave the flat with a couple of hours to spare before we have to leave for the airport. This time I don't care who sees me walking with Serge as we carry my bags to his flat.

Serge insists on taking me to the airport. As we leave the compound, I switch my phone off. About 10 kilometres from the compound Serge's phone rings. It is Mona, phoning from the palace on behalf of the princess to tell me that the driver is at the compound door waiting to take me to the airport. Mona is the only person who knew I would be with Serge, so after trying my phone, the logical step would be to try his.

He hands me the phone and I tell her that no arrangements were made with me about transport to the airport, so she should tell the princess I am in a cab on my way as we speak. Before I kill the call, I cannot help adding, "If it will further your cause at all, tell the princess that my passionate Lebanese lover is taking me to the airport." Serge looks at me incredulously, laughing hard.

A sombre mood sets in again after the brief humorous moment. As we stop at the various sets of traffic lights, Serge just looks at me. I see the same torment I am feeling in his eyes. Initially we don't talk, each lost in finding ways to cope with the loss. Words would have shattered the intimacy, so we just hold hands. He lifts my hand to his mouth and holds it against his lips.

As we reach the airport, Serge says gently, "Habibty, I will take you." From that moment on, I watch with adoration as he takes care of everything.

He hands in my luggage as we both pass through the first set of security gates. Serge goes through the metal arch with other men as I follow the queue of women who pass through a curtain, into a room where two women search my handbag. My little ruby belly ring sets off the alarm. After hitching my abaya up and showing them the culprit, they smile and wave me through. Thank goodness I exchanged belly rings.

I meet Serge on the other side, where he leads me through the crowds towards the food court. We put in our order and he gently asks me if I need the bathroom, points it out and shows me where to find him in the dining area afterwards. I am in a bit of a haze and allow myself to be led.

We settle in at the family section in a cubicle that affords us some privacy. This is my first time in a restaurant in Saudi in the family section with a man unrelated to me, as I'm leaving.

He opens my cold drink can, inserts the straw, and hands it to me. The food tastes like cardboard and sticks to my palate. Everything is happening in slow motion. We have very few words.

After our dinner, Serge reaches for my hand as we slowly walk back outside the busy terminal. A bold move but what the hell, what can they do to me now, deport me?

He stops a cab driver walking past offering his fare, and asks him to take a photograph of us. The smiles aren't genuine. Eventually we move inside only for my belly ring to set the alarm off again. Once again my abaya is lifted. The same two women don't recognise me until they see my exposed stomach.

The time has come. I want to bury myself in his arms but I can't. Holding hands is one thing; overly emotional displays of affection are sure to draw attention. I pull my abaya over my head and give it to Serge. "Keep it for me until I come and claim it back." My attempt at humour fails miserably.

The greeting is almost formal but I know what Serge is feeling by the way he is shaking as we hug each other – probably a little longer than we should. He stands back; keeping his hands on my shoulders, and tells me earnestly that he will leave the airport only after my flight has taken off. All I can do is nod. He gives me a last quick crushing hug and turns around and walks towards the stairs leading to the glass enclosure on the first floor.

For a moment, I just stand there, watching him walk away.

I am forced to move on as the throng of people behind me is struggling to pass. Every couple of seconds, I turn to see him, just 30 metres away, looking down at me through the glass barrier, one moment, smiling and the next, looking intense. As I join the queue, I can still see him. I bump into people as I am forced forward but I keep looking back.

He phones me and across King Khalid airport, we declare our love for one another. His voice breaks as we say goodbye. I see his head drop to his chest as we end the call. The memory of it will be forever burnt into my mind.

The queue passes along to a point where he is now out of sight. He phones again, just to repeat his choked declaration of love. The people behind me discreetly look the other way as the tears start. I am so choked up I can't talk, only listen. As I reach the final exit leading outside, I turn for the last time and for the briefest moment I see him in the distance, with his arm raised high above his head. Then he is gone.

Epilogue

EVEN THOUGH I am exhilarated to be going home, for many reasons my heart is heavy when I board the plane.

I wholeheartedly believe that this is the best ending to a life-changing experience for all concerned. Yet, it has become such a part of life to me that without it, I feel momentarily bereft.

I feel privileged to have met some wonderful people. Even with all the restrictions, the Saudis' hospitality is legendary. Experiencing Saudi Arabia first hand has been an incredibly enriching experience.

As for the princess, we have had no contact since I left. I hear from a reliable source, six months later, that three PAs have made their way hastily home since my departure.

I believe God gave me the protection I asked for, when I was sitting on the plane with my head bowed.

This is by no means meant to be a love story but at the same time, I cannot underplay the beautiful experience God had chosen to bestow on me. My own Lawrence of Arabia, on the gate with cake.

— 237 —

I will mourn the cats for a very long time to come. How many of them go days without eating, living in summer temperatures relentlessly hovering near 50 degrees day after day. I torture myself with images of Mr Grey waiting at the compound's gate. How long before he gives up . . .

Glossary

habibti – Darling to a female

Habibi – Darling to a man

Shukran – Thank you

Khalas – Finished

Awrah – Parts of the body not meant to be exposed

Abaya – Full black cloak worn as an outer garment over clothing

Hijab – Black scarf that covers the head

Nigab – Veil covering the face

Mahram – Anyone a Muslim is not allowed to marry is *mahram*

Purdah – A sharp separation between the world of men and women

Apostasy – Falling away, defecting from, forsaking or departing from the faith

Haram – Forbiddden

Halal – Allowed

Ghutra – men's scarf made of cotton or silk

Infidels – Non-believers

Insha'Allah – God willing

Masha'Allah – Praise to God (or thank God)

Al-hamdu lillāh – Praise to God

Badawi – Bedouin-Arab word – desert-dweller

Mafi mushkila – No problem

Zakat – Giving charity